FUCK JESUS

Exposing the hateful, vengeful, and ignorant nature of Jesus using His own words and works

by Judas H. Peters

Fuck Jesus by Judas H. Peters is licensed under a Creative Commons Attribution-NonCommercial-ShareAlike 4.0 International License.

https://creativecommons.org/licenses/by-nc-sa/4.0/

You are free to:

Share — copy and redistribute the material in any medium or format

Adapt — remix, transform, and build upon the material

Under the following terms:

Attribution — You must give appropriate credit, and indicate if changes were made.

Non-Commercial — You may not use the material for commercial purposes.

Share-Alike — If you remix, transform, or build upon this material, you must distribute your contributions under the same license as the original.

ISBN-13: 978-1514211274
ISBN-10: 1514211270

All biblical passages come from the King James Bible (emphasis mine). All other text by Judas Peters

Cover art includes *The Crucifixion* by Alonzo Cano (1638)

Contact:
judashpeters@gmail.com
Twitter: @fuckjesusbook
www.fuckjesusbook.blogspot.com/
Facebook: https://www.facebook.com/FJesusBook

10 9 8 7 6 5 4 3 2 1

Acknowledgments

I am eternally grateful to all of my Christian friends and family, youth ministers, priests, popes, and elders, who have helped me understand that we are all much better than Jesus.

To My Liberal-Christian Friends

This book is for you. You have taught me that your hearts are true, your intentions are good, and you want nothing but the best for our world. We all agree that the Old Testament God is a monstrous devil, but for some reason we disagree on the nature of Jesus.

Throughout my life, you have all taught me to be good, to seek justice, to right wrongs, and to change the world. You all taught me that this was what Jesus stood for. Unfortunately, when I read the Gospels as an adult, I realized that Jesus stood for the exact opposite: he sought revenge, not justice; He wanted to perpetuate wrongs, not right them; He wanted to keep the world the way it was, not change it for the better. I pray that you read this book and discover the same wretched Jesus I discovered on my own journey.

To My Atheist Friends

This book is for you. You have taught me that your hearts are true, your intentions are good, and you want nothing but the best for our world. We agree that the Old Testament God is a monstrous devil, but some of us disagree on the nature of Jesus.

For some reason, I hear far too many of you say things like, "sure, Jesus was a kind man who said some really amazing things..." But Jesus wasn't kind - He was a complete jerk. And His teachings weren't amazing - they were completely awful.

I present to you over one hundred of Jesus' worst teachings, words, and actions so that you will never again feel obligated to perpetuate the lie that Jesus was "good".

To My Ultra-Conservative Christian Friends

This book is not for you. I know that you don't care what kind of a monster or hypocrite you worship.

Fuck Jesus: Inspired by God

I was an atheist sitting in the pews with my extended family, in the winter of 2014, listening to a preacher give his passionate Christmas sermon. He was obviously discussing the Christmas story, one I had heard every year since I could remember. But until that evening I had never grasped the dark subtext of the story.

When the preacher came to the part of the story where the angels warned the wise men to avoid Herod, I finally realized the horrific irony of the story: the slaughter of the innocents was planned by God.

I had never realized before how much divine intervention there had been: The angel appearing to Mary; the angel appearing to Joseph to calm his nerves; angels appear to shepherds to tell them about baby Jesus; angels appear to the wise men to warn them not to go back to Herod; an angel appears to Joseph to warn him of Herod preparing to kill the children in Bethlehem.

I realized then that heavenly warnings were used quite often in preparing the way for Baby Jesus, and in fact relied upon such heavenly interference. And it was at that moment, in Church, that I realized that there was one specific intervention that was conveniently left out: warning the wise men NOT to visit Herod in the first place.

Had the wise men never sought Herod's help in looking for Jesus, Herod would have never sent out orders to kill all of the children under two. When I realized that sparing the lives and suffering of the children and their parents was never part of God's plan, I remember thinking to myself in my loudest thought ever:

"Fuck Jesus"

So, this book was conceived in a Christian church, during Christmas Mass, inspired by the words of God and His minister.

Structure of the Page

In order to present the most user-friendly book as possible, I have structured the pages in a specific format. This format, I believe, will allow the reader to not only enjoy reading the book, but will also allow the reader to use this book as a useful tool for quickly accessing information when in a discussing, or when arguing the nature of Jesus' words and actions.

Please see the diagram below and the text on the following page for an explanation of the page structure.

 Matthew 17:19-20

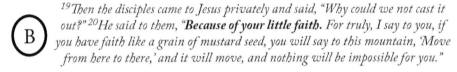
[19]Then the disciples came to Jesus privately and said, "Why could we not cast it out?" [20]He said to them, "**Because of your little faith.** For truly, I say to you, if you have faith like a grain of mustard seed, you will say to this mountain, 'Move from here to there,' and it will move, and nothing will be impossible for you."

Surely the disciples have more faith than a mustard seed because they have been doing all of the work that he has asked them to do. They have been successfully casting out demons, healing people, and other miraculous works.

Jesus likes to berate people and use his power to make them feel small. So, when his disciples ask him why their magic doesn't work, Jesus takes the opportunity to tell them that it is all their fault.

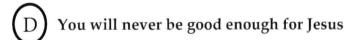 **You will never be good enough for Jesus**

 *See also:*
Luke 17:5-10

A: Bible verse - The Bible verse is presented centered at the top of the page for quick reference when discussing this content with Christian apologists or interested Atheists.

B: Bible text - The text of the verse is presented from the Authorized King James Edition (KJV). While the KJV is often criticized for being more difficult to understand, I have done so only for reasons of copyright. Sometimes more text is included so that the specific verses are presented in a bit more context. The reader is always encouraged to read and re-read as much of the original text as desired. For additional help, I have included my own emphasis in order to highlight the most important parts of each page.

C: Commentary - After presenting the original KJV text, I include my own abbreviated commentary to further argue how the selected verse shows that Jesus is not as wonderful as originally thought.

Often times when discussing the Bible with Christians, I am told that I am not reading the Bible verses "in context". In order to curtail that argument from Christian readers, when appropriate, I use this section to go into further detail to provide even more context for the selected verse.

D: Moral - In order to make to make it as easy as possible for the reader to flip through the book to find the most useful information possible, I have included a single bold moral statement to summarize each page.

This was a later addition to book. As I was editing this text, I found myself wanting to glean the content of each page as quickly as possible. I realized that by adding a summarizing statement at the bottom of each page, I made this book much easier to use as a discussion aid.

E: Because many of the events and stories are repeated within the four gospels, instead of repeating my own text, I have provided references to where the story is told in the other gospels. Most often, these references are almost exact retelling of the stories. In a few cases, the references are to stories or events that are just very similar.

STRUCTURE OF THE BOOK

This book focuses exclusively on The Gospels of Matthew, Mark, Luke, and John. Because the four gospels often repeat stories and events, I have restructured the information presented in this book, which, I believe, makes for a more pleasurable and understandable reading experience.

First, I have organized the text into major themes (e.g. The Baby, The Miracles, The Parables, etc). In this way, when reading straight through this book, even though events aren't presented linearly according to time, Jesus' words and actions according to each theme will make much more sense, will reinforce each other, and are presented in better context than they are in the original New Testament.

Within each theme, I attempt to present the selected verses in chronological order, instead of presenting the verses in the order they appear in The Bible. In some cases, it was very easy to understand how the verses occurred chronologically, in other cases the time-line was less understandable. However, while the time-line I present may not be perfect, it is a very good representation of the order of events.

Some of the verses may seem to fall within multiple themes, such as when Jesus performs a miracle while admonishing his disciples. In these cases, I simply made a choice based on number of entries within each theme.

In this way, I have attempted to make it as easy as possible for you to retrieve the information you desire. If you want to recall one of Jesus' specific responses to the Pharisees, you only need to flip to the chapter on the Pharisees and read chronologically, instead of first figuring out which Gospel and where within the Gospel the verse would be.

Contents

The Baby 11

The Preparation 15

The Pharisees 21

The Disciples 35

The Miracles 47

The Evangelists 63

The Gospel 81

The Parables 125

The Deception 151

The Index 161

Fuck Jesus

I
The Baby

(Where we learn that Jesus planned Herod's slaughter of the innocents.)

Matthew 1:17

*So all the generations **from Abraham to David** are fourteen generations; and **from David** until the carrying away into Babylon are fourteen generations; and from the carrying away into Babylon **unto Christ** are fourteen generations.*

The first book of the New Testament begins by detailing Jesus' lineage, which is meant to showcase Jesus' familial connection to Abraham and David. There are two problems with this.

First, the story completely leaves out Mary's lineage and only focuses on Joseph's. Considering that Joseph has nothing to do with Jesus' conception (as far as we know), this lineage is both pointless and confusing. It is also as if Mary is completely disregarded (as Jesus disregards her later in *John 2:4*, and *Matthew 12:47-50*).

Second, the focus on lineage reminds us that Jesus only came for the Jews (as Jesus himself will remind people as he begins his ministry in *Matthew 10:5-6* and *Matthew 15:22-26*). The lineage of Jesus reiterates the importance of a bloodline, rendering all who are not of the bloodline unimportant and unworthy.

Lineage and bloodline are important

See also:
Luke 3:23-38

Fuck Jesus

Matthew 1:18

Now the birth of Jesus Christ was on this wise: When as his mother Mary was espoused to Joseph, **before they came together,** *she was found with child of the Holy Ghost.*

Because Mary was in her early teens and still only engaged to Joseph when she was asked to become impregnated with the Messiah, Jesus' plan from the very beginning put people's lives in danger and was much more complicated than it needed to be.

While *Deuteronomy 22:13-21* allows for a man to murder his new bride if she's not a virgin, it is interesting to note that Joseph disregarded those teachings of his Holy book, and instead opted to follow the much more rational path of letting his child-bride live. It was only after this time that an angel finally decided to let Joseph in on the God-impregnation plan.

This problem could have been avoided altogether if Joseph was told about the plan directly after Mary accepted to take part in it. However, this lack of foresight is merely a foreshadowing of many more incidents of poor planning skills of Jesus Christ.

It could also be noted here that being born of a virgin isn't even terribly miraculous, since a woman can become pregnant through non-intercourse activities (Google it).

Lastly, this plan condones the concept of child-brides since the angels came to Mary while she was in her early teens. While some apologists claim that Jesus shouldn't be blamed since this was the culture at the time, Jesus is not known for succumbing to cultural norms, so He wouldn't have begun his ultimate plan using a child-bride unless he condoned the practice.

Jesus is a very poor planner

Matthew 2: 1-3

¹Now when Jesus was born in Bethlehem of Judaea in the days of Herod the king, behold, there came wise men from the east to Jerusalem, ²Saying, Where is he that is born King of the Jews? for we have seen his star in the east, and are come to worship him. **³When Herod the king had heard these things, he was troubled,** *and all Jerusalem with him.*

It should be very telling that Jesus' entrance into the world came with the murder of many innocent little children - a foreshadowing of Jesus' perpetuation of the idea of suffering (*Luke 6:21*), his admonishing of pleasure (*Luke 6:25*), and his teachings about not caring about your family (see index: "family").

In the first place, the wise men were allowed to visit Herod to inquire about a "King of the Jews", which ensured that Herod was alerted to the potential threat to his throne. In order for Jesus' life to be saved, however, the wise men were miraculously told by an angel to avoid Herod on their way back. This bought Jesus and his family the time they needed to get out of town, right before Herod murdered every single child under two years of age.

The wise men could have received a vision telling them to avoid Herod in the first place, but that wasn't part of Jesus' plan. The plan, for some reason, had to involve many murdered children, and probably the wailing and gnashing of teeth of the parents of the murdered children.

Jesus is a baby murderer

II
THE PREPARATION

(Where we learn that Jesus hates the family, and loves torture.)

Luke 2:48-49

⁴⁸*And when they saw him, they were amazed: and his mother said unto him, Son, why hast thou thus dealt with us? behold, thy father and I have sought thee sorrowing.* ⁴⁹*And he said unto them,* ***How is it that ye sought me? wist ye not that I must be about my Father's business?***

When Jesus was a child, He disappeared, which caused Mary and Joseph to spend three days looking for Him. When they finally found him, Jesus seemed to completely disregard their feelings, saying to them:

> *How is it that ye sought me? wist ye not that I must be about my Father's business?*

Jesus' callous response to his worried mother and father is another indication of the fact that Jesus had either no idea or no concern for normal human emotion. He didn't let his family know that he would be hanging out in the Temple for so long, he didn't send an angel to let them know that He was alright, He didn't say He was sorry, and He didn't seem to care about the torment and anguish that Mary and Joseph must have been feeling.

Jesus doesn't care about family's suffering

Matthew 3:11-12

11　*I indeed baptize you with water unto repentance: but he that cometh after me is mightier than I, whose shoes I am not worthy to bear: he shall baptize you with the Holy Ghost, and with fire:* **12** *Whose fan is in his hand, and he will throughly purge his floor, and gather his wheat into the garner;* **but he will burn up the chaff with unquenchable fire.**

John the Baptist is referring to Jesus in this passage, and the reader should note that John states that Jesus will gather the wheat, but will burn the chaff with a fire that cannot ever be extinguished.

While this is essentially a metaphor, it is specifically meant as a scare tactic, to instill fear and terror into the lives of those who follow John. John specifically mentions an "unquenchable fire" that will be burning up the chaff.

From the beginning, Jesus has his reputation solidified as someone who will not only come for and reward his followers, but who will also vengefully and psychotically torture non-believers forever in an unquenchable fire.

Jesus could, if He wanted to, annihilate unbelievers in an instant, snuffing them out instantly and painlessly. But He instead opts for a much more disturbing technique: endless torture.

Jesus wants to torture unbelievers

Matthew 4:11

*Then the devil leaveth him, and, behold, **angels came and ministered unto him**.*

After being baptized by John, Jesus embarks on a trip to the desert in order to fast and meditate.

After a long time of starving His body of essential nutrients, Jesus experiences Satan coming to him to tempt him with all sorts of wonderful things. Instead of giving in to temptation, Jesus resists and is rewarded with angels ministering to his needs.

Here we see that Jesus, a deity, needs special assistance from heavenly angels in order to restore him back to his normal self. While it is a difficult thing to do, other prophets from the Bible completed the task (Moses and Elijah), and they weren't deities.

Jesus' need for and use of angels in this passage foreshadows Jesus' constant double-standard of expecting humans to be stronger and smarter than Himself. Whether it is Jesus rebuking humans for not performing enough miracles (*Matthew 17:14-17*), admonishing humans for not understanding cryptic and confusing messages (*Matthew 16:11*), or commanding us to be perfect (*Matthew 5:48*), Jesus constantly holds humans to either the same or higher standards than that which He holds for Himself.

Jesus is weaker than humans

John 2:3-4

³*And when they wanted wine, the mother of Jesus saith unto him, They have no wine.* ⁴*Jesus saith unto her,* **Woman, what have I to do with thee?** *mine hour is not yet come.*

The above interaction occurs during a wedding, right before Jesus turns water into wine, which is often referred to as Jesus' first miracle, and hailed as a symbol of how much Jesus condones marriage.

This particular moment, however, shows Jesus clearly breaking the fourth or fifth (depending on which brand of Christianity you follow) commandment to honor one's mother and father. First, Jesus calls his mother "woman", which was a way of distancing himself from her, almost as a way of disowning her as a mother at that point. Second, even though Jesus eventually does what she asks, at first he's adamantly against it, and refuses.

This also shows Jesus clearly stating something that is unflattering, and then changing His mind, possibly to deal with the resulting public opinion (such as when he calls a gentile woman a dog in *Matthew 15:21-28*). At first Jesus brushes off Mary's suggestion to help the wedding, perhaps because He values marriage so little (Jesus will eventually tell his followers to abandon their wives and children in *Matthew 19:29*). It is only later, perhaps when he saw people giving him dirty looks, that he reluctantly helped out with the wedding the way his mother asked.

Jesus treated his mother with disdain

III
THE PHARISEES

(Where we learn that Jesus delights in deceiving us in how to follow God's law.)

Mark 2: 27-28

²⁷And he said unto them, The sabbath was made for man, and not man for the sabbath: **²⁸*Therefore the Son of man is Lord also of the sabbath.***

After the Pharisees ask Jesus why he and his disciples picked ears of corn on the Sabbath (thereby "working" on the Sabbath, which was forbidden), Jesus' response is essentially, "because we wanna."

By saying this, Jesus is disregarding the third or fourth commandment (depending on which brand of Christianity you follow) to keep the Sabbath holy. In *Numbers 15:32-36* God mandates the death penalty for working on the Sabbath:

> *And the LORD said unto Moses, The man shall be surely put to death: all the congregation shall stone him with stones without the camp.*

Not only was Jesus violating his own Father's commandment, the actual excuse he gives is ridiculous. In *Mark 2:25-26* Jesus states that they are allowed to break laws because when King David was hungry, he also broke some of the laws of God.

But David wasn't perfect - he murdered a man in order to get with the man's wife, so how can Jesus cite such him to base his morality on? It should be obvious to the reader that Jesus was caught being imperfect, and so tried to make up an excuse on the spot. It didn't work, so he ended with the verse above - he could do whatever he wanted, similar to the childish retort: "nyah nyah."

Jesus violates God's rules

See also:
Matthew 12:1-8
Luke 6: 1-5

Matthew 12:38-39

38 *Then certain of the scribes and of the Pharisees answered, saying, Master, we would see a sign from thee.* **39** *But he answered and said unto them,* ***An evil and adulterous generation seeketh after a sign;*** *and there shall no sign be given to it, but the sign of the prophet Jonas:*

While the Pharisees did oppose Jesus, and were trying to entrap him, it is easy to see from the last example why it was that they considered Jesus to be a heretic rather than the Son of their God.

For how did Jesus think he was going to convince the religious leaders that he was from their God, by going against the rules of their God? Jesus gave them no reason to believe that he was the Son of God, and yet when the Pharisees ask for a sign, a signal, a reason to believe, He gives them nothing.

Instead of helping them realize who He is, Jesus tells them not only that they will receive a sign only when it is too late, but that they are evil and adulterous, too.

Jesus seems to expect people to believe in him, while not giving then any reason to other than his word. By doing this, Jesus is essentially damning believers to Hell, their only sin being that they wanted to be sure that they placed their faith in a true prophet.

Jesus deceives you

See also:
Luke 11:29-32

Luke 13: 14-15

¹⁴*And the ruler of the synagogue answered with indignation, because that* **Jesus had healed on the sabbath day**, *and said unto the people, There are six days in which men ought to work: in them therefore come and be healed, and not on the sabbath day.* **¹⁵** *The Lord then answered him, and said, Thou hypocrite, doth not each one of you on the sabbath loose his ox or his ass from the stall, and lead him away to watering?*

Jesus admonishes the ruler of the synagogue for following God's rules. Much like the way he previously chastised the Pharisees for following God's rules, Jesus here is ridiculing the ruler of the synagogue for actually obeying the law that God (Jesus' supposed Father) gave humans in the first place.

When put in this perspective, it is hard to understand why Jesus is so angry with the Pharisees and others who are trying to obey God.

Jesus will continue to violate God's laws, refuse to show people that he is God's Son, and yet still become angry and confused as to why people don't realize he is the Son of God.

Jesus violates God's rules

See also:
Luke 14:1-6

Matthew 15: 3-6

³*He answered them, "And why do you break the commandment of God for the sake of your tradition?* ⁴*For God commanded, 'Honor your father and your mother,' and, **'Whoever reviles father or mother must surely die.'** * ⁵*But you say, 'If anyone tells his father or his mother, "What you would have gained from me is given to God,"* ⁶*he need not honor his father.' So for the sake of your tradition you have made void the word of God.*

When the Pharisees ask Jesus about breaking the tradition of the elders, Jesus replies by asking why the Pharisees honor tradition over obeying God. Jesus specifically references the commandment to honor one's father and mother, and even more specifically mentions the death penalty for not obeying that command.

An apologist might discuss this particular quote from Jesus as having more to do with pointing out hypocrisy than with killing children. They might point out that in context, Jesus took this opportunity to mention how the Pharisees have become corrupt and that their man-made rules are ungodly.

However, Jesus specifically mentions the death penalty, and specifically reiterates that He believes that the commandments are very important to keep, including killing children.

Jesus encourages killing children

Also see
Mark 7:1-13

Matthew 15:10-11

¹⁰*And he called the people to him and said to them, "Hear and understand:* **¹¹***it is not what goes into the mouth that defiles a person****, but what comes out of the mouth; this defiles a person."*

Jesus speaks the verses above after the Pharisees admonish Jesus and his disciples for not washing their hands before they eat. Jesus could have taken a moment to discuss germs and infections in order to save countless people in the future from epidemics, but instead taught that washing hands isn't important.

Of the children in the world suffering from diarrhea (deadly in many parts of the world) The Centers for Disease Control and Prevention (CDC) estimate that washing hands can save one third of them. Of the children around the world suffering from Pneumonia, washing hands can save one sixth.

Instead of helping people with real problems, Jesus spouts figuratively about something that is literally untrue.

Jesus doesn't know or care about germs

Also see:
Mark 7:14-23
Luke: 11:37-41

Fuck Jesus

Matthew 16:1-3

¹*And the Pharisees and Sadducees came, and to test him they asked him to show them a sign from heaven.* ²*He answered them, a "When it is evening, you say, 'It will be fair weather, for the sky is red.'* ³*And in the morning, 'It will be stormy today, for the sky is red and threatening.'* **You know how to interpret the appearance of the sky, but you cannot interpret the signs of the times.**

Jesus seems to think that the esoteric ramblings of the prophets are just as clear to humans as a red sky in the morning or evening.

When my own mother told me long ago that a red sky in the morning is bad news, and that a red sky at night is a "delight", it made so much sense that I couldn't do anything to forget it. Jesus makes fun of the "red skies" as signs, yet the red skies are more understandable, more predictable, and more relatable than any sign ever given from God.

What Jesus still doesn't understand or care about is that He wants people to both believe the signs of the Bible, but to also disbelieve the Bible when Jesus breaks its laws.

Jesus is delusional about his signs

Also see:
Mark 8:11-13
Luke 12:54-56

Matthew 16:21

*From that time forth began Jesus to shew unto his disciples, how that **he must go unto Jerusalem, and suffer many things of the elders and chief priests and scribes, and be killed,** and be raised again the third day.*

From the beginning, Jesus has planned it out so that he must suffer by the hands of the elders. Perhaps this is why Jesus is not actually helping the Pharisees understand who he is. And if this is the case, then he is actively forcing them to want to kill him, since His Father sent commandments to kill false prophets (*Deuteronomy 13:1-5*).

And so it follows that if Jesus was actively trying to make it so that the Pharisees and elders didn't believe He was Son of God, then Jesus is also a deceiver.

What else has Jesus deceived us about, in order to carry out a plan that few understood? And will Jesus deceive people in the future in order to carry out yet another ill-conceived far-fetched plan?

Jesus deceives you

See also:
Mark 8:31
Luke 9:21-22

John 5:39-43

39 *Search the scriptures; for in them ye think ye have eternal life: and they are they which testify of me.* **40** *And ye will not come to me, that ye might have life.* **41** *I receive not honour from men.* **42** *But I know you, that ye have not the love of God in you.* **43** ***I am come in my Father's name, and ye receive me not****: if another shall come in his own name, him ye will receive.*

Jesus is annoyed that people study the scriptures and come to the conclusion that Jesus isn't the Messiah. But from the beginning, Jesus has been disregarding and contradicting God's laws in the first place. It is also in the scriptures that you should kill false prophets (*Deuteronomy 13:1-5*).

This is a wonderful little catch-22 that goes something like this: If you read the scriptures, then you should see that the scriptures point to Jesus being Son of God. But, if we are to believe that Jesus is the Son of God, then we should believe his words. Since Jesus has stated that the scriptures aren't correct (such as regarding working on the Sabbath) then we are to believe that the scriptures are flawed, and we might not believe that the signs do point to Jesus.

But, this would mean that Jesus isn't the Son of God, which would mean we could believe the scriptures once again.

This must be why, in *Matthew 18:1-3*, Jesus will tell people that you have to go to Jesus like a child - as someone who hasn't studied all of the scriptures yet, and who has little grasp of logic and rationality.

Do AND don't read scripture

John 5:46-47

⁴⁶*For had ye believed Moses, ye would have believed me:* *for he wrote of me.*
⁴⁷But if ye believe not his writings, how shall ye believe my words?

Jesus oddly states that if people believed Moses, then they would surely believe that Jesus is the Messiah. This is odd because Jesus is putting confidence in Moses' words, and is suggesting people should believe what Moses had to say.

However, in *Matthew 19:8*, Jesus openly states that we shouldn't believe Moses, specifically regarding divorce.

This opens up a fun Catch-22 where if we believe Jesus, then we should not put too much faith in Moses. But if we don't put faith in Moses, then by Jesus' statement above, we wouldn't believe in Jesus.

And if we don't believe in Jesus, then we can go ahead and put our faith back in Moses, which, according to Jesus, would mean that we should have to believe in Jesus again.

Does your head hurt yet?

Believe Moses AND don't believe Moses

Luke 17:20-21

[20]*And when he was demanded of the Pharisees, when the kingdom of God should come, he answered them and said,* **The kingdom of God cometh not with observation:** [21]*Neither shall they say, Lo here! or, lo there! for, behold, the kingdom of God is within you.*

Jesus must have forgotten that he had already admonished people (*Matthew 16:1-3*) for not seeing the signs of the coming of the Kingdom of God.

Here, Jesus states that there will be no signs. This is an example showing that Jesus doesn't really have too much of a plan, that he is forgetful about what he's stated previously, and that he just makes things up as he goes, without caring whether it contradicts previous statements or not.

Jesus is contradictory

Matthew 19:7-8

⁷ *They [Pharisees] said to him, "Why then did Moses command one to give a certificate of divorce and to send her away?"* ⁸ *He said to them, "**Because of your hardness of heart Moses allowed you to divorce your wives**, but from the beginning it was not so.*

The Pharisees are once again trying to trick Jesus into saying things that will get him into trouble, and Jesus is once again trying to avoid it even though His entire plan rests being killed for the wild and crazy things he says.

But if Jesus states that Moses was wrong, then what else was Moses wrong about, and when was Jesus going to let us in on that little secret?

The entire time that elapsed from Moses until right then had existed with the Israelites believing that divorce was acceptable. But now, Jesus states that, "actually, Moses was wrong." But why didn't God ever speak up? Jesus' response to that question is to claim that God let it go because remaining married was too hard for people back then.

If we are to believe Jesus, then we are to believe that the same God who allowed people to divorce even when He didn't want divorce, was the same God who demanded people kill those who pick up sticks on the Sabbath.

Divorce okay - death for picking up sticks

Matthew 21:24-27

²⁴*And Jesus answered and said unto them, I also will ask you one thing, which if ye tell me, I in like wise will tell you by what authority I do these things.* ²⁵*The baptism of John, whence was it? from heaven, or of men? And they reasoned with themselves, saying, If we shall say, From heaven; he will say unto us, Why did ye not then believe him?* ²⁶*But if we shall say, Of men; we fear the people; for all hold John as a prophet.* ²⁷*And they answered Jesus, and said, We cannot tell.* And he said unto them, Neither tell I you by what authority I do these things.

Jesus consistently refuses to tell people that he is the Son of God, while actively telling people that they will burn forever in hell for not believing that he is the Son of God.

Because Jesus doesn't placate the Pharisees, he doesn't provide any of us with any reason for believing. To the question of whether Satan was giving Jesus His powers - Jesus never states otherwise. If the religious leaders at the time couldn't fathom that Jesus was getting his powers from God (or a version of Himself) then why should we?

Jesus essentially does all of humanity a disservice by not answering this question. The very frustrating part of this is that Jesus at this time is actually quite close to being betrayed when He is questioned here, so maybe Jesus could have spared Judas the horrible task of betrayal if He had just been honest instead.

Jesus abhors honesty

See also:
Mark11:27-33
Luke 20:1-8

III The Pharisees

John 8:43-47

⁴³Why do ye not understand my speech? *even because ye cannot hear my word.* ⁴⁴*Ye are of your father the devil, and the lusts of your father ye will do. He was a murderer from the beginning, and abode not in the truth, because there is no truth in him. When he speaketh a lie, he speaketh of his own: for he is a liar, and the father of it.* ⁴⁵*And because I tell you the truth, ye believe me not.* ⁴⁶*Which of you convinceth me of sin? And if I say the truth, why do ye not believe me?* ⁴⁷*He that is of God heareth God's words: ye therefore hear them not, because ye are not of God.*

It is funny to me that the above verses represent just a really long rant of Jesus circularly arguing how those who are against him are essentially idiots.

The response to Jesus' initial question "why do ye not understand my speech?" can be summed up with Jesus' own words in *John 16:25*:

> *These things have I spoken unto you in proverbs: but the time cometh, when I shall no more speak unto you in proverbs, but I shall shew you plainly of the Father*

So Jesus admits that He doesn't speak to people plainly but is astonished that people don't understand His words. He knowingly confuses people that He knows cannot understand his words, and gets annoyed with their lack of understanding. Perhaps if Jesus wanted people to understand Him, He would learn how to communicate with the humans He supposedly had a hand at creating.

Jesus deliberately confuses you

IV

The Disciples

(Where we learn that Jesus enjoys tormenting and antagonizing those who follow Him.)

Matthew 8: 21 - 22

²¹*And another of his disciples said unto him, Lord, suffer me first to go and bury my father.* ²²*But Jesus said unto him, Follow me; and* **let the dead bury their dead.**

Jesus spent the first thirty-two years of his life preparing to teach his gospel. When he finally gets the gumption to go look for disciples, one potential disciple says that has to bury his father and Jesus tells him to forget his dead father and abandon the body (Jesus was evidently in a hurry).

If you have ever lost a loved one, Jesus' command here may be a bit hard to take. Jesus is forcing the disciple to sever his emotional ties to his father, to abandon the feelings he has for his father so that he can join up with and travel with Jesus.

Notice Jesus didn't tell the potential disciple that he should be with his family and mourn the loss of the person who raised him, and to meet up with Jesus later. Hence, this is another window for us to see what Jesus thinks of family: Jesus doesn't think people should mourn for their parents, take care of their bodies, or even help comfort other survivors.

Jesus doesn't care about your family, just as He already showed us that He doesn't care about his own family.

Don't mourn the loss of your parents

See also:
Luke 14:25-33

Mark 4:37-40

³⁷*And there arose a great storm of wind, and the waves beat into the ship, so that it was now full.* ³⁸*And he was in the hinder part of the ship, asleep on a pillow: and they awake him, and say unto him, Master, carest thou not that we perish?* ³⁹*And he arose, and rebuked the wind, and said unto the sea, Peace, be still. And the wind ceased, and there was a great calm.* ⁴⁰*And he said unto them,* **Why are ye so fearful? how is it that ye have no faith?**

Jesus and the disciples are on a boat at sea when a storm comes. As the storm is beating the ship, Jesus is asleep and doesn't seem to be waking up. Eventually, after the disciples realize that Jesus isn't going to wake up on his own, the disciples wake him.

Jesus' response to this is to berate their lack of faith. But, in the disciples' defense, Jesus was sleeping while the storm was tormenting the ship. All of the evidence showed that they needed to wake Jesus up to tell him about the storm.

After all, they have eyes to see the storm, and ears to hear the storm, why should they not wake Jesus to help calm the storm? Imagine if they had let the storm continue to damage the ship until it destroyed it - I can just imagine Jesus' response:

> *Why are ye so foolish? Why didn't you fools wake me to calm the storm? How is it that ye have no faith?*

Jesus admonishes you for fearing for your life

See also:
Matthew 8:23-27
Luke 8:22-25

Matthew 14:28-31

²⁸*And Peter answered him and said, Lord, if it be thou, bid me come unto thee on the water.* ²⁹*And he said, Come. And when Peter was come down out of the ship, he walked on the water, to go to Jesus.* ³⁰*But when he saw the wind boisterous, he was afraid; and beginning to sink, he cried, saying, Lord, save me.* ³¹*And immediately Jesus stretched forth his hand, and caught him, and said unto him,* **O thou of little faith, wherefore didst thou doubt?**

Here is another instance where Jesus takes a moment to remind his disciples how horrible they are. Peter actually has the most faith out of all of his fellow disciples: he risks his life to perform an action that should go against every ounce of rationality that a human should have, and he walks on water.

Sure, when the wind becomes more boisterous, Peter becomes a little more scared and a little more concerned for his life. But for Peter to sink, one of two things must be happening.

Either Jesus is in full control of Peter's miracle and decides to yank away the walk-upon-water strength as his faith lessens, or Peter has the power to walk on water himself, in which case we can all do such a feat if we have enough faith.

Since no one has ever managed to walk on water since this story, we have to assume that Jesus Himself took away Peter's ability to walk on water as his faith lessened, (which actually helped reduce Peter's faith even more-so). After-all, what kind parent hugging a scared child through a thunderstorm, doesn't hug even tighter when the child becomes more scared at the loudest cracks of thunder? Only an evil parent would loosen their grip and say, "I thought you trusted me! Faithless child!"

Jesus does not appreciate your faith

Matthew 16:11

How is it that you fail to understand that I did not speak about bread? Beware of the leaven of the Pharisees and Sadducees."

In *Matthew 16*, The disciples realize that they have forgotten to bring bread with them on their little jaunt, and Jesus interrupts with a warning about the leaven from the Pharisees. So when the disciples talk with each other, trying to figure out if Jesus is talking about literal or figurative bread, Jesus admonishes them about not understanding that he was speaking figuratively.

Jesus often gets annoyed with his disciples for not understanding his words, so much so that one would think that Jesus would begin speaking in plainer words. Instead, Jesus continues speaking allegorically, cryptically, and esoterically and continues to curse and admonish people for not understanding Him.

(Just before he dies, in *John 16:25*, Jesus does mention that He will eventually speak in plainer language, but I guess he died too soon to actually carry that plan out.)

Jesus deliberately confuses you

Matthew 16:22-23

²²*And Peter took him aside and began to rebuke him, saying, "Far be it from you, Lord! This shall never happen to you."* ²³*But he turned and said to Peter,* **"Get behind me, Satan! You are a hindrance to me.** *For you are not setting your mind on the things of God, but on the things of man."*

Directly before this moment, Jesus commends Peter for having faith in Him. Unfortunately, Peter continues to express that he wants Jesus to stay alive, and so Jesus calls Peter "Satan".

Remember that people in those days were used to their God repaying their good works and faith with Earthly kingships and actual thrones, and with breaking free from actual bondage and servitude. So it should be surprising to people that Jesus, Himself, is surprised that people expect Him to bring an actual return to the throne.

It is funny to note that the opposite of Peter's position would be to be accepting of Jesus' death. But if you were to accept Jesus' death, then you would find it odd that Jesus kept avoiding crowds, authorities, and tried to remain in the shadows.

Judas, then, by helping Jesus' plan come to fruition, represents the opposite of Peter's position here. But instead of rewarding Judas' part in helping Jesus' plans, in *Luke 22:3*, Jesus states that Judas' actions were also from Satan.

You will never be good enough for Jesus

See also:
Mark 8:31-33
Luke 9:21-22

Matthew 17:14-17

¹⁴*And when they came to the crowd, a man came up to him and, kneeling before him,* ¹⁵*said, "Lord, have mercy on my son, for he is an epileptic and he suffers terribly. For often he falls into the fire, and often into the water.* ¹⁶*And I brought him to your disciples, and they could not heal him."* ¹⁷*And Jesus answered,* **"O faithless and twisted generation, how long am I to be with you? How long am I to bear with you?** *Bring him here to me."*

Jesus is absolutely fed up with humans for a couple of reasons. First, Jesus seems to hate it when people don't understand when He is being literal or figurative. Second, Jesus is constantly reprimanding his disciples for not having enough faith.

But his disciples do have faith, and they have healed many people at this point (supposedly). And if anyone is making the disciples lose any faith, it is probably because Jesus is constantly speaking esoterically, and admonishing his disciples for not having enough faith.

Let me repeat Jesus' words:

> *O faithless and twisted generation, how long am I to be with you? How long am I to bear with you?*

Jesus hates spending time with you

See also:
Mark 9:14-19
Luke 9:37-41

IV The Disciples

Matthew 17:19-20

¹⁹ *Then the disciples came to Jesus privately and said, "Why could we not cast it out?" ²⁰ He said to them, "**Because of your little faith.** For truly, I say to you, if you have faith like a grain of mustard seed, you will say to this mountain, 'Move from here to there,' and it will move, and nothing will be impossible for you."*

Surely the disciples have more faith than a mustard seed because they have been doing all of the work that he has asked them to do. They have been successfully casting out demons, healing people, and other miraculous works.

Jesus likes to berate people and use his power to make them feel small. So, when his disciples ask him why their magic doesn't work, Jesus takes the opportunity to tell them that it is all their fault.

You will never be good enough for Jesus

See also:
Luke 17:5-10

Matthew 21:21-22

²¹And Jesus answered them, "Truly, I say to you, **if you have faith and do not doubt,** you will not only do what has been done to the fig tree, but even if you say to this mountain, 'Be taken up and thrown into the sea,' it will happen. **²²**And whatever you ask in prayer, you will receive, if you have faith."

Jesus sets us up to only blame ourselves and our lack of faith if we are not able to accomplish a goal, or if we do not receive what we pray for.

On the surface this sounds good. If you believe in Jesus, you can ask for something and it will be given, or it will be done. So if you ask why there are Christians starving around the world, the answer has to be that every Christian who prays for the end of starvation is severely lacking in faith.

The same can be said for suffering in general: surely Christians who suffer ask for and pray for God to ease pain and suffering. According to Jesus in this passage, the answer has to be that it is the fault of the people who are in pain and suffering, for not having enough faith.

It's your fault if you suffer

Luke 22:3-4

³***Then entered Satan into Judas surnamed Iscariot**, being of the number of the twelve.* ⁴*And he went his way, and communed with the chief priests and captains, how he might betray him unto them.*

While Jesus' plan was to die at the hand of the elders and authorities, he spend much of his time hiding the shadows to avoid being caught (*John 7:6-9*).

If Satan is involved in this plan, it is because it is Jesus' plan to use Satan: Jesus could have preached openly; He could have told people He was God or the Son of God; He could have healed the masses instead of hiding from them; He could have done all of this and more.

But no, he chose instead to work with Satan to make Judas do something so horrible that he would eventually kill himself over it.

Jesus works hand-in-hand with Satan

Matthew 26:24-25

²⁴*The Son of man goeth as it is written of him:* **but woe unto that man by whom the Son of man is betrayed!** *it had been good for that man if he had not been born.* ²⁵ *Then Judas, which betrayed him, answered and said, Master, is it I? He said unto him, Thou hast said.*

Jesus concocted a plan that involved Judas betraying Him and delivering Jesus to the authorities for money. This is Jesus' plan, yet He chastises the very human who helps that plan occur.

Think about how it may have seemed from Judas' point of view: Jesus states that He shall be killed as a sacrifice; Peter objects and Jesus calls him "Satan" (*Matthew 16:23*); Jesus hides from authorities to not be caught (*John 7:6-9*); Jesus chastises his own disciples for not understanding His cryptic words (*Matthew 16:11*).

Since Jesus refuses to just speak plainly, to the point that his disciples rarely understand him, it is entirely possible that Judas thought he was actually helping Jesus' own plan be carried out.

To help prove my point, in *Matthew 26:56*, after Judas brings the authorities to Jesus, Jesus states:

> *But all this was done, that the scriptures of the prophets might be fulfilled.*

Following Jesus' plans can damn you to Hell

See also:
Mark 14:12-21
Luke 22:7-13
John 13:18-30

Fuck Jesus

V

THE MIRACLES

(Where we learn that (among other things) Jesus doesn't really want to heal or help you.)

Mark 1:44-45

44And [Jesus] saith unto him, **See thou say nothing to any man:** *but go thy way, shew thyself to the priest, and offer for thy cleansing those things which Moses commanded, for a testimony unto them.* **45** *But he went out, and began to publish it much, and to blaze abroad the matter, insomuch that Jesus could no more openly enter into the city, but was without in desert places: and they came to him from every quarter.*

Directly after healing lepers, Jesus clearly instructs them to not tell anyone so that He won't be bothered by massive crowds.

This passage makes it clear, based on Jesus' decision to avoid the crowds of people who desired to be healed, that He didn't want to spend too much time actually helping or healing people in the first place.

This idea is supported by the use of the word "But" in *Mark 1:45* - the sentence goes on to explain the repercussions that Jesus was hoping to avoid: He could no longer "openly enter into the city".

So, Jesus was essentially swamped with undesirables - the people that he and God allowed to become sick in the first place. And instead of dealing with their infirmities, Jesus hides out in desert places to avoid them as much as possible.

Jesus doesn't want to heal you

See also:
Matthew 8:1-4
Luke 5:12-16

Matthew 8: 31 - 34

31 *So the devils besought him, saying, If thou cast us out, suffer us to go away into the herd of swine.* **32** *And he said unto them, Go. And when they were come out, they went into the herd of swine: and, behold,* **the whole herd of swine ran violently down a steep place into the sea, and perished in the waters.** **33** *And they that kept them fled, and went their ways into the city, and told every thing, and what was befallen to the possessed of the devils.* **34** *And, behold, the whole city came out to meet Jesus: and when they saw him, they besought him that he would depart out of their coasts.*

Jesus travels to Gergesenes, casts demons out of one man, and into a herd of swine, which sends them into the sea, killing them.

The people who herded those swine were not very happy about this 'miracle', since Jesus essentially killed all of the swine. This shows that Jesus ruins property, and also submits to the wishes of demons, since Jesus could have sent them back to hell if he wanted to. This is definitely a case of a miracle gone wrong.

Jesus is a swine killer

See Also:
Mark 5:1-20
Luke 8:26-39

Luke 7:11-14

11*And it came to pass the day after, that he went into a city called Nain; and many of his disciples went with him, and much people.* **12***Now when he came nigh to the gate of the city, behold, there was a dead man carried out, the only son of his mother, and she was a widow: and much people of the city was with her.* **13*****And when the Lord saw her, he had compassion on her,*** *and said unto her, Weep not.* **14***And he came and touched the bier: and they that bare him stood still. And he said, Young man, I say unto thee, Arise.*

This passage supports the idea that Jesus only has compassion for people when He sees them in person. For instance, Jesus will only feel moved to heal people who are standing right in front of Him. If He knows that people need healing in a city, and He is perhaps on the outskirts of town away from their sight, then He really doesn't care to help them.

For instance, in this story Jesus has compassion on the woman who's son has died, so he raises the son from the dead. But she is certainly not alone in losing an only son. There must have been many others at that time, and there have been countless others throughout the rest of history, yet Jesus doesn't have compassion on anyone else losing their only sons.

If Jesus thinks that it is important and helpful to keep people's children alive, then perhaps He doesn't know about all of the children dying right at this very moment, the parents of whom desperately call out for His miracles.

Jesus was on Earth for a brief moment of time, and was forced to see individuals, and has since forgotten us.

Jesus doesn't care about your sorrow

Matthew 9:20 - 22

²⁰ And, behold, *a woman, which was diseased with an issue of blood twelve years*, *came behind him, and touched the hem of his garment:* **²¹** *For she said within herself, If I may but touch his garment, I shall be whole.* **²²** *But Jesus turned him about, and when he saw her, he said, Daughter, be of good comfort; thy faith hath made thee whole. And the woman was made whole from that hour.*

We tend to think of these miracles as really nice stories, where Jesus comes to Earth and kindly and generously helps everyone out because he's a really swell guy.

The problem is, if Jesus and His Father are one, then they're the ones who invented the system where this poor woman has been bleeding for the twelve years prior to Jesus gracing her with His presence. Did she not pray about the legion within those twelve years? Did God listen?

So Jesus lets the woman bleed for twelve years, and only heals her because she happened to reach out and grab his clothes.

Jesus won't be troubled to help you

Luke 8:49-50

⁴⁹*While he yet spake, there cometh one from the ruler of the synagogue's house, saying to him, Thy daughter is dead; trouble not the Master.* ⁵⁰*But when Jesus heard it, he answered him, saying, Fear not:* **believe only, and she shall be made whole.**

Jesus' lack of clarification in the words above has caused many deaths in our modern world. Numerous people who believed that Jesus wouldn't lie to humans have fallen for the "believe only, and she shall be made whole" blather.

Probably the most well-known case in the US of people following Jesus' horrible advice on healing is the Schaible family of Philadelphia, Pennsylvania, where it is legal for parents to follow Jesus' outlandish philosophy on healing.

The couple's first child died in 2009 from pneumonia because the parents relied on Jesus' gospel: they believed only, and refused medical treatment. The couple's second child died in 2013 from diarrhea and breathing problems, since the parents again believed in Jesus' gospel.

The parents clearly believed that Jesus would heal their children, otherwise, they would have sought minimal medical attention, which would more than likely have saved their children from Jesus' neglect.

Jesus' words kill children

Matthew 11:5

The blind receive their sight, and the lame walk, the lepers are cleansed, and the deaf hear, the dead are raised up, **and the poor have the gospel preached to them.**

Jesus' miraculous powers may work for some parlor tricks, but when it comes to being poor, Jesus' only recourse is to preach.

In the end they are still poor, because Jesus cannot or will not heal or solve poverty.

Jesus can't or won't solve poverty

See also:
Luke 7:18-23

Mark 3:9-12

⁹*And he spake to his disciples, that a small ship should wait on him because of the multitude, lest they should throng him.* **¹⁰***For he had healed many; insomuch that they pressed upon him for to touch him, as many as had plagues.* **¹¹***And unclean spirits, when they saw him, fell down before him, and cried, saying, Thou art the Son of God.* **¹²***And he straitly charged them that they should not make him known.*

Jesus tells his disciples to make sure that he has a boat ready so he can keep enough distance between Himself and the people who want to be healed. The text here seems to suggest that Jesus didn't want to heal the people who had come to see Him, so he needed to put distance between him and the people.

Aside from the fact that Jesus suggests that he is not powerful enough to not be trampled by the crowd, aside from the fact that Jesus suggests that he needs a boat to stand on water and can't do it on his own (can't walk on water?), aside from the fact that Jesus suggests that he doesn't have the power to keep people from moving on their own; this passage points out the fact that, once again, Jesus is letting us know that he does not actually want to heal people.

The healing that Jesus actually does take part in is merely a by-product of his real mission: To let people know that he is going to throw people into Hell.

Jesus doesn't want to heal you

Matthew 13:54-58

⁵⁴*And when he was come into his own country, he taught them in their synagogue, insomuch that they were astonished, and said, Whence hath this man this wisdom, and these mighty works?* ⁵⁵*Is not this the carpenter's son? is not his mother called Mary? and his brethren, James, and Joses, and Simon, and Judas?* ⁵⁶*And his sisters, are they not all with us? Whence then hath this man all these things?* ⁵⁷*And they were offended in him. But Jesus said unto them, A prophet is not without honour, save in his own country, and in his own house.* ⁵⁸***And he did not many mighty works there because of their unbelief.***

If Jesus wanted to show his family and friends in His hometown that He was actually the Son of God, then He could have showed them. Instead, Jesus was insulted by their unbelief and decided not to bother helping them understand, letting them fall to the punishment He so desires: burning people alive forever.

Jesus constantly blames other people for their unbelief, when it is his own failure to prove Himself that is the real culprit. Perhaps if He spoke clearly and offered proof, then He would inspire the belief that He so truly desires.

Jesus here essentially does as little as he can to help save his hometown, and when it comes time to help the people believe in Him, He abandons them instead.

Jesus will abandon you

See also:
Mark 6:1-6
Luke 2:39-40
Luke 4:16-30

Matthew 15:22-26

22And behold, a Canaanite woman from that region came out and was crying, "Have mercy on me, O Lord, Son of David; my daughter is severely oppressed by a demon." **23**But he did not answer her a word. And his disciples came and begged him, saying, "Send her away, for she is crying out after us." **24**He answered, **"I was sent only to the lost sheep of the house of Israel."** **25**But she came and knelt before him, saying, "Lord, help me." **26**And he answered, **"It is not right to take the children's bread and throw it to the dogs."**

At this point in Jesus' ministry, He is openly stating that He only came for the Jews. So when a non-Jew comes to Jesus, He calls her a dog. And since Jesus hates dogs (*Matthew 7:6*), this is meant to insult the woman, showing us that Jesus is actually mean and insensitive.

The woman eventually gets Jesus to realize that she is not a dog, and ends up making Jesus look like a jerk in front of people who still think He's a nice guy. So, in order to save face, Jesus finally concedes to heal her child.

Unfortunately, Jesus doesn't take this moment to instruct people about the non-existence of demons.

Jesus didn't care about non-Jews

See also:
Mark 7:24-30

Matthew 15:30-31

³⁰*And great crowds came to him, bringing with them the lame, the blind, the crippled, the mute, and many others,* **and they put them at his feet, and he healed them,** ³¹*so that the crowd wondered, when they saw the mute speaking, the crippled healthy, the lame walking, and the blind seeing. And they glorified the God of Israel.*

Great crowds glorified God because Jesus came and healed a few people from a fate that was given to them by the same God in the first place.

If you believe in God, then you must believe this: God makes it so that people are born deaf or blind into a culture that hates these qualities in people; at some point in time, God sends down his Son to fix a few of the people who suffered from the fate, which makes people thank God.

This is like when a builder builds a house for you, with three of the walls missing. The builder then sends his son to put up two more walls, leaving one whole side of the house open to the elements. People who do that are called incompetent cons.

Jesus partially repairs His Father's mistakes

Matthew 15:36-38

36 *he took the seven loaves and the fish, and having given thanks he broke them and gave them to the disciples, and the disciples gave them to the crowds.* **37** *And they all ate and were satisfied. And they took up seven baskets full of the broken pieces left over.* **38** *Those who ate were four thousand men, besides women and children.*

Jesus can always make food appear to feed an unlimited number of people, yet allows countless people across the globe, across all of time, to starve and die from hunger.

But this story actually reveals another aspect of Jesus that few people ever talk about. Most of the liberal Christians I know use this story of feeding the multitudes to showcase how Jesus cares about feeding the hungry. But, if you read the story in context, then you realize that Jesus doesn't advocate feeding the hungry, he was merely feeding *these* hungry people.

Jesus never uses his miraculous multiplying powers to feed people who are starving, or to help ease the toiling and strife of those who hunger every day. In fact, Jesus is an advocate of suffering on a daily basis: being fed in Heaven, not while on Earth. So every liberal Christian who is feeding the homeless - they aren't actually following Jesus' example, because Jesus would have stayed far away and let them starve.

Jesus didn't feed the hungry

See also:
Mark 8:1-10

Matthew 21:18-19

18 *In the morning, as he was returning to the city, he became hungry.* **19** *And seeing a fig tree by the wayside, he went to it and found nothing on it but only leaves. And he said to it,* **"May no fruit ever come from you again!"** *And the fig tree withered at once.*

First, this passage shows that Jesus is not miraculously all-knowing. Second, this shows how angry and ticked off Jesus can get at things that no one should get mad about.

Jesus isn't just a little angry here, he actually curses a non-sentient being. And not only that, but Jesus makes this poor plant die. The tree actually withers and dies. If this is how Jesus treats plants, I'd hate to see what he might do to a human. Oh right, He tells us: He will throw us into the fires of hell to burn forever.

Jesus is irrationally angry (God hates figs)

See also:
Mark 11:12-14
Mark 11:20-26

Matthew 28:17

And when they saw him, they worshipped him: ***but some doubted***

After Jesus rises from the dead and gathers his disciples together, some of them doubt that He is actually Jesus.

Knowing that even his close followers at the time doubt that Jesus rose from the dead, why should Jesus constantly threaten us with eternal damnation for our own disbelief?

Although, reflecting on the fig incident (*Matthew 21:18-19*), we know that Jesus is irrationally angry, so it actually might make sense that Jesus would damn us for making such a rational choice.

Jesus' resurrection was doubtful

See also:
Mark 16:14

John 9:1-3

¹*And as Jesus passed by, he saw a man which was blind from his birth.* ²*And his disciples asked him, saying, Master, who did sin, this man, or his parents, that he was born blind?* ³*Jesus answered, Neither hath this man sinned, nor his parents:* **but that the works of God should be made manifest in him.**

While Jesus suggests here that deformities do not come from sin, in *John 5:14*, Jesus insinuates that deformities do, in fact, come from one's sins.

What's worse, Jesus suggests here that people are born blind so that Jesus and His followers can show how awesome God is by healing them. If people were born disabled so that Jesus could use them as props to gain followers, why were people born disabled before Jesus, and why are people born disabled now that Jesus gone?

Jesus considers the disabled as props

Fuck Jesus

VI
THE EVANGELISTS

(Where we learn that Jesus wants you to abandon your family and suffer)

Matthew 10:5-6

⁵ *These twelve Jesus sent forth, and commanded them, saying,* **Go not into the way of the Gentiles, and into any city of the Samaritans enter ye not:** ⁶ *But go rather to the lost sheep of the house of Israel.*

As seen in *Matthew 15:22-26,* Jesus is pretty clear that he really doesn't care about non-Jews.

Jesus didn't care about non-Jews

Matthew 10:7-8

⁷And as ye go, preach, saying, The kingdom of heaven is at hand. ⁸Heal the sick, cleanse the lepers, raise the dead, cast out devils: freely ye have received, freely give.

Here we see Jesus essentially instructing his disciples on what to tell people about Jesus and his mission to save the world, and all we get is, "The Kingdom of Heaven is at hand."

What does that even mean? Flash forward 2000 years later, and we still have religious fundamentalists claiming that the end of the world is coming. Jesus doesn't tell his disciples to teach people to act kind, to start helping the needy, to help the poor, or anything like that.

Jesus instructs his disciples that they should heal, cleanse, raise the dead and deal with demons. One thing has always struck me: why raise the dead? Jesus came to open the gates of Heaven, AND he forced his disciples themselves to abandon their newly-deceased loved-ones' bodies. So, why make a big fuss about raising the dead?

Also, these are all band-aid solutions. Jesus could have taught his disciples to go out and teach people about germs, psychotherapy, medicine, and other things. But instead, he charges them with fixing the biological mistakes of His Father.

Jesus' gospel is ridiculous

Matthew 10: 14-15

14*And whosoever shall not receive you, nor hear your words, when ye depart out of that house or city, shake off the dust of your feet.* **15***Verily I say unto you,* ***It shall be more tolerable for the land of Sodom and Gomorrha*** *in the day of judgment, than for that city.*

It is important to note a few things about Jesus at this point: Jesus has just begun His ministry; Jesus just finished killing someone else's pigs (*Matthew 8: 31 - 34*); Jesus keeps telling people to not share news that he heals them (*Mark 1:44*); Jesus' teachings contradict God's laws (*Mark 2: 27-28*).

So Jesus gives little reason for anyone to believe that He is the Son of God, yet he is going to damn entire cities to be burned by fire and brimstone because they don't want to blindly believe a few strangers who show up with no food, money or even the Messiah they claim to represent.

Jesus, essentially, chooses to punish rational judgment with utter annihilation.

Jesus punishes rationality

See also:
Mark 6:7-13
Luke 9:4-6
Luke 10:10-12

Matthew 10: 16-18

¹⁶*Behold, I send you forth as sheep in the midst of wolves: be ye therefore wise as serpents, and harmless as doves.* ¹⁷*But beware of men: for they will deliver you up to the councils,* **and they will scourge you in their synagogues**; ¹⁸*And ye shall be brought before governors and kings for my sake, for a testimony against them and the Gentiles.*

In this passage we are given some insight into Jesus' plan for the dissemination of His message: His whole plan this entire time involves having His messengers being chased out of their cities and even killed.

One alternative for Jesus is to make the message easier to believe: Jesus could clone Himself, or actually be the messenger as the resurrected Christ; He could go back in time and change the Old Testament prophesies to make more sense; He could give the messengers special powers so that they won't be put to death.

This also shows that Jesus didn't die in place of us, because he expects Christians to die BECAUSE of him. Remember that because Jesus' plan involved people not believing Him and putting Him to death, Jesus HAD to ensure that most people didn't believe in Him.

Unfortunately for evangelizing Christians, this means that it is very difficult to believe in Jesus, unless you suspend your own rationality, like a child (*Matthew 18:1-3*). This, combined with the fact that God commanded His people to kill false prophets and heretics, Jesus has ensured that his followers will surely be murdered for following His words.

Jesus wants you to be murdered

Matthew 10:34-37

³⁴ *Think not that I am come to send peace on earth: I came not to send peace, but a sword.* ³⁵ *For I am come to set a man at variance against his father, and the daughter against her mother, and the daughter in law against her mother in law.* ³⁶ *And a man's foes shall be they of his own household.* ³⁷ **He that loveth father or mother more than me is not worthy of me: and he that loveth son or daughter more than me is not worthy of me.**

Anyone who thinks that Jesus stands for family values should re-read this part of the Bible. Here Jesus clearly states that His followers are going to have to sever ties with their family members.

Even if Jesus is over-emphasizing with the word "hate", the general impression is that you will have to either leave your family, stop talking to your family, want to kill your family, deny your family, or other type of action that is essentially against the family unit.

Perhaps Jesus doesn't understand what real familial love is, since Jesus' own Father used him in a weird twisted plot to murder Him.

Jesus doesn't value family

See also:
Luke 12:49-53

Matthew 11:20-22

20 *Then began he to upbraid the cities wherein most of his mighty works were done, because they repented not:* **21** *Woe unto thee, Chorazin! woe unto thee, Bethsaida! for if the mighty works, which were done in you, had been done in Tyre and Sidon, they would have repented long ago in sackcloth and ashes.* **22** *But I say unto you,* ***It shall be more tolerable for Tyre and Sidon at the day of judgment, than for you.***

Here is a perfect example of when Jesus should sit down and relax for a bit. Jesus absolutely hates it when people are skeptical about Messianic claims. And for their acts of skepticism, Jesus is going to rain down hellfire upon them.

But Jesus fails to understand why skepticism is so valuable. Jesus has already made it clear that he wants people to be gullible and believe Him without proof or evidence.

But if someone were to believe Jesus or Jesus' disciples without evidence, then why is it unacceptable to believe in another religion without evidence. Or, when the anti-Christ comes, why is it unacceptable to be "fooled" by the anti-Christ?

Jesus fails to understand that He actually should want people to demand proof from a Messiah, so that we can distinguish the real from the fake.

Jesus doesn't want you to use your mind

Luke 10:16

*He that heareth you heareth me; and he that despiseth you despiseth me; and **he that despiseth me despiseth him that sent me.***

It is completely unfair of Jesus to suggest that people are rejecting God if they choose to reject Jesus.

To reiterate: Jesus deliberately broke laws that God told his people to follow (*Mark 2: 23-28*); Jesus is deliberately wishy-washy about who he is (*Matthew 27:11*); Jesus continuously hides his identity (*Matthew 12:38-39*); Jesus continuously and deliberately speaks cryptically and esoterically (*Matthew 13:10-11*); and when Jesus is asked directly to prove He is the Son of God, he refuses and gives lame excuses.

If people despise Jesus, it is only because people are actually trying to follow His Father's rules. Unfortunately, God is such a tyrant that people are completely afraid of following the wrong rules, and both God and Jesus are making it terribly difficult for people to figure out what to do in this case.

Jesus is unfair

Matthew 11: 29

Take my yoke upon you, and learn of me; ***for I am meek and lowly in heart:*** *and ye shall find rest unto your souls.*

Jesus claims to be meek, which means "quiet" or "gentle". Is this the term to describe someone who demands that his followers renounce and hate their families, or leave their parents' bodies to rot?

Is "meek" the word you would use to describe someone who would send you to burn forever in hell if you couldn't believe He was the Son of God?

Jesus is a liar

Matthew 11: 30

For my yoke is easy*, and my burden is light.*

Jesus claims that his yoke is easy, yet just a few moments before he states this, he tells the disciples that they must: travel without money (*Matthew 10:9*); travel without shoes or staffs (*Matthew 10:10*); and rely on strangers for lodging (*Matthew 10:11-13*).

In addition to that, Jesus also states that he is sending them "as sheep in the midst of wolves" (*Matthew 10:16*) for they will be delivered up before authorities, they will be persecuted, and they will be killed (*Matthew 10:17-23*).

This doesn't sound like an easy yoke to me.

Jesus is a liar

Matthew 12:32

And whosoever speaketh a word against the Son of man, it shall be forgiven him: **but whosoever speaketh against the Holy Ghost, it shall not be forgiven him,** *neither in this world, neither in the world to come.*

Jesus seems to indicate here that he will forgive you if you speak against Him. However, I'm not sure how much stock you should put into that statement since He just finished telling the disciples that he will annihilate and destroy any town that doesn't want to listen to the disciples.

But, even if you do believe what Jesus says now about people speaking against Him, there is something seriously wrong about the second portion of this verse: If you speak against the Holy Ghost then you will never ever ever ever be forgiven.

Of course, the Holy Ghost is actually the hardest of the trinity to believe in. Yahweh (God, Jehovah, Allah, whomever) is the main character in the Old Testament and Jesus is the main character in the New Testament. But we barely know who or what the Holy Ghost (aka Holy Spirit) even is, and y et we will never be forgiven if we speak against it (him? her?).

Jesus is unfair

See also:
Luke 12:10

Matthew 12:47-50

47 Then one said unto him, Behold, thy mother and thy brethren stand without, desiring to speak with thee. **48** But he answered and said unto him that told him, **Who is my mother? and who are my brethren? 49** And he stretched forth his hand toward his disciples, and said, Behold my mother and my brethren! **50** For whosoever shall do the will of my Father which is in heaven, the same is my brother, and sister, and mother.

More "family values" lessons from Jesus: Jesus takes a moment here to remind his followers that THEY are now his "mother and brethren", that they are the same to him as his mom and siblings.

Unless you're a mother or father, you might not understand how this might hurt. It's really not about Mary being "better" than anyone of his followers, it is about the fact that she's his MOM! She risked her own life for him, brought him up, fed him and clothed him, and now that he is an adult, he feels he can disown her in front of his followers.

Value your cult over your real family

Matthew 13:57-58

*⁵⁷And they were offended in him. But Jesus said unto them, A prophet is not without honour, save in his own country, and in his own house. ⁵⁸**And he did not many mighty works there because of their unbelief.***

When Jesus is confronted with people who know Him, yet who don't believe that He is the Son of God, He makes a sarcastic remark and then gives up and leaves.

When faced with unbelievers, that is the BEST time to perform amazing miracles to help them believe. Instead, Jesus lets them remain in their unbelief, securing their fates to wail and gnash their teeth in the furnaces of hell.

Jesus is a lazy evangelist

See also:
Luke 4:16-30

John 6:26-27

26 *Jesus answered them and said, Verily, verily, I say unto you,* **Ye seek me, not because ye saw the miracles, but because ye did eat of the loaves, and were filled.** **27** *Labour not for the meat which perisheth, but for that meat which endureth unto everlasting life, which the Son of man shall give unto you: for him hath God the Father sealed.*

Jesus is chastising people for being hungry and wanting to be fed. If this is Jesus' attitude, perhaps he shouldn't have placed us in a universe where we need food to survive. Jesus here understands that the physical ache of hunger is present in these people who seek him, yet he chooses to admonish them for bowing to such a silly reason.

After the Israelites fled Egypt and wandered the desert, Moses' God was able to provide sustenance for His people in the form of manna. Jesus, on the other hand, can't seem to comprehend what hunger is, and why people are hungry.

Jesus doesn't care if people are actually hungry or starving, he's not the kind of God who will actually feed one's stomach. But, if you are starving to death, Jesus is the kind of God who, if you believe in him, will feed you spiritually, while you are dying of hunger.

Jesus doesn't care about the hungry

John 7:6-9

⁶ *Then Jesus said unto them, My time is not yet come: but your time is alway ready.* ⁷ *The world cannot hate you; but me it hateth, because I testify of it, that the works thereof are evil.* ⁸ *Go ye up unto this feast:* ***I go not up yet unto this feast; for my time is not yet full come.*** ⁹ *When he had said these words unto them, he abode still in Galilee.*

Shortly after many disciples abandon Jesus due to his lack of proof of being the Son of God, Jesus' brothers suggest that he preach and perform miracles out in the open so that people will know who He is.

Jesus' response above, however, is a lie. Jesus seems to indicate that he will operate in the open when his time will come, but Jesus continues to avoid crowds and hide in secrecy his entire career. Again, his entire plan COULD have been for him to preach and perform miracles in public, but instead Jesus chooses to hide in secret so his best friend Judas would turn him in, which ultimately affected Judas so much that he killed himself.

Jesus lied to hide from his responsibility

Matthew 28:18-20

¹⁸And Jesus came and spake unto them, saying, All power is given unto me in heaven and in earth. **¹⁹Go ye therefore, and teach all nations,** *baptizing them in the name of the Father, and of the Son, and of the Holy Ghost:* **²⁰***Teaching them to observe all things whatsoever I have commanded you: and, lo, I am with you alway, even unto the end of the world. Amen.*

Jesus has died, risen, and has gathered his disciples together into the mountain side to talk to them one final time.

The issue with this scenario is that Jesus himself has stated numerous times that He cannot trust His own disciples to understand the Gospel that Jesus came to Earth to preach (*Matthew 16:11*). And now that Jesus is dead and has the ability to walk the Earth preaching His own gospel, He leaves that mission to His faulty, limited, slow-witted disciples.

If Jesus really wanted to have his message spread properly, He would have done it Himself. It is clear that Jesus not only could care less about having his message accurately reach people, but that He must have wanted people to not receive His message, so that He could throw people into the fires of hell.

Jesus wants to obfuscate His message

See also:
Mark 16:15-18

Mark 16:17-18

17 *And these signs shall follow them that believe; In my name shall they cast out devils; they shall speak with new tongues;* **18** ***They shall take up serpents; and if they drink any deadly thing, it shall not hurt them;*** *they shall lay hands on the sick, and they shall recover.*

Jesus' careless words here have led to the deaths of many people who believed that Jesus was actually telling the truth.

In the US, there are groups of people who follow Jesus' words, by holding poisonous snakes, since Jesus taught that believers will "take up serpents" and not be hurt. People in these sects of Christianity don't realize that Jesus was either wrong or was lying.

The most recent example as of this writing was Pastor Jamie Coots, who died of a snakebite in 2014. A couple of years before that, Pastor Mark Wolford died of a snakebite as well. According to the Encyclopedia of Occultism and Parapsychology, "less than 75 deaths have been recorded as of the mid-1990s."

While this is not a very high number compared to other dangers (less than one death per year), they are deaths nonetheless, proving that Jesus was careless with his words.

Jesus' lies can kill you

Mark 16:20

And they went forth, and preached every where, **the Lord working with them, and confirming the word with signs following.** *Amen.*

Directly after Jesus dies, His disciples go out to tell people about Jesus, and Jesus evidently follows them and is able to provide proof to people through signs, saving them from an eternity of burning alive forever in Hell.

Unfortunately for us, at some point Jesus realized that providing signs as proof of his deity doesn't allow him to torture as many people, so he has since stopped following his evangelists and has ceased providing signs.

Jesus won't give us signs

VII
The Gospel

(Where we learn that Jesus wants you to suffer on
Earth as well as in Hell)

Matthew 5:3

³Blessed are the poor in spirit: *for theirs is the kingdom of heaven.*

Here, Jesus is showing us that he doesn't care how we suffer here on Earth because he believes that things are going to be better in Heaven. If we are sad or sorrowful, Jesus' words are meant to keep us from wanting to make our lives better here on Earth, when we're alive, since, as he suggests, we are "blessed" to be poor in spirit.

Jesus here is similar to an ego-maniacal abuser. He wants us to be ashamed of ourselves, believing that we are not even fit to strap Jesus' sandals. He wants us to be sorrowful, sad, and feeling down. He doesn't want us to be happy, or rejoice-full.

Jesus wants you to be sorrowful

See also:
Luke 6:20-21

Luke 6:21

Blessed are ye that hunger now: *for ye shall be filled.* **Blessed are ye that weep now:** *for ye shall laugh.*

Jesus is supporting living a life of unfulfilled hunger. There is another layer of interest here, considering that the Pharisees had recently chastised Jesus and his disciples for their own lack of fasting (*Matthew 9:14-15*): Jesus preaches living with hunger, yet He Himself lives a life of satisfying his own hunger.

Unfortunately, Jesus' attitude here is not acceptable. We should live our lives to fulfill our dreams - accepting the permanence of hunger is a defeatist attitude that may have served well a population that accepted living in bondage, but not for a free civilized society.

Additionally, by creating the dichotomy of weeping vs. laughing, Jesus is planting a seed of accepting a sorrowful life without rebelling for a greater, happier tomorrow.

Jesus wants you to starve / Jesus hates your laughter

See also:
Matthew 5:4

Luke 6:24-26

²⁴But woe unto you that are rich! for ye have received your consolation. ²⁵ Woe unto you that are full! for ye shall hunger. **Woe unto you that laugh now!** *for ye shall mourn and weep. ²⁶ Woe unto you, when all men shall speak well of you! for so did their fathers to the false prophets.*

Jesus is essentially damning anyone who has any inkling of a good life on Earth. He is telling us that having money is bad, eating food on a regular basis is bad, and yes, even laughing is bad!

Again, Jesus has no vision for solving the world's problems. He could never have envisioned that humanity could surpass the wretched lives that people in his day led, and he shows his ignorance here.

Jesus wants you to live in sorrow and agony

Matthew 5:17-19

17 *Think not that I am come to destroy the law, or the prophets: I am not come to destroy, but to fulfil.* **18** *For verily I say unto you,* **Till heaven and earth pass, one jot or one tittle shall in no wise pass from the law,** *till all be fulfilled.* **19** *Whosoever therefore shall break one of these least commandments, and shall teach men so, he shall be called the least in the kingdom of heaven: but whosoever shall do and teach them, the same shall be called great in the kingdom of heaven.*

Apologists will often suggest that Jesus isn't actually suggesting that every "jot" and "tittle" of the law needs to be followed, that Jesus is just saying that the laws will still be on the books, so to say, but that people don't have to follow them.

They say this because many atheists and critics will suggest that this passage means that the laws about refraining from shellfish (*Leviticus 11:12*), are still in place, and that Christians who eat shellfish are sinning just as much as those engaging in homosexual activities (*Leviticus 20:13*).

However, if you keep reading through to *Matthew 5:19*, you see that Jesus specifically states that we do, in fact, need to keep the commandments, and refrain from breaking even the least of them.

Jesus could have said, "love each other unconditionally." But instead, he said that we have to keep the laws, which includes killing people who work on Sunday (*Numbers 15:32-36*).

Jesus wants you to kill people who work on Sunday

See Also:
Luke 16:17

Matthew 5:21-22

²¹*Ye have heard that it was said by them of old time, Thou shalt not kill; and whosoever shall kill shall be in danger of the judgment:* ²²*But I say unto you, That **whosoever is angry with his brother without a cause shall be in danger of the judgment:** and whosoever shall say to his brother, Raca, shall be in danger of the council: but whosoever shall say, Thou fool, shall be in danger of hell fire.*

Jesus is essentially criminalizing our emotions. While we cannot dictate our emotions, we can learn how to deal with our emotions properly. Instead of praising people for handling emotions in a civilized way, Jesus tells us that he will monitor our brain and punish us for thought-crimes.

Jesus is right about the fact that we shouldn't get angry, but He is also saying that if we do become angry, that it is quite possible that Jesus will burn us alive forever in the pits of Hell.

Jesus will punish you for thought-crimes

Matthew 5:27-28

²⁷Ye have heard that it was said by them of old time, Thou shalt not commit adultery: ²⁸But I say unto you, That **whosoever looketh on a woman to lust after her hath committed adultery** with her already in his heart.

Our creator gives us a brain that actually is wired to think about sex, yet Jesus comes along and wants to punish us for thinking about it.

Again, Jesus is going to burn people alive forever in Hell for thought-crimes.

Jesus will punish you for thought-crimes

Matthew 5:29 - 30

²⁹*And **if thy right eye offend thee, pluck it out**, and cast it from thee: for it is profitable for thee that one of thy members should perish, and not that thy whole body should be cast into hell.* ³⁰*And **if thy right hand offend thee, cut it off**, and cast it from thee: for it is profitable for thee that one of thy members should perish, and not that thy whole body should be cast into hell.*

This is a terrible solution for two reasons. First, the hand doesn't make people do bad things. If you steal something or hurt someone with your hand, chopping it off will not stop you from stealing or hurting someone again - it will not change your character.

Additionally, according to Jesus' own words, if you even think about a sin that you would take part in if you did have a body part, you are just as guilty as if you had done that sin (*Matthew 5:27-28*). So, chopping off a body part, even if it does help you not take part in the sin, will not help you anyway.

Second, it suggests that we enter into Heaven with our deformities.

Jesus advocates unnecessary self-mutilation

See also:
Matthew 18:9
Mark 9:43-48
Luke 17:1-4

Matthew 5:31 - 32

³¹ *It hath been said, Whosoever shall put away his wife, let him give her a writing of divorcement:* ³² *But I say unto you, That* ***whosoever shall put away his wife, saving for the cause of fornication, causeth her to commit adultery:*** *and whosoever shall marry her that is divorced committeth adultery.*

Jesus here makes it very obvious that He does not want us to change our minds about who we have married. He additionally mentions that He's very interested in people's sex lives by telling us the only reason for getting a divorce: fornication.

Jesus doesn't care if there is spousal abuse, or even if both parties mutually decide to leave each other.

Hence, Jesus is forcing lifelong monogamy onto us, and claiming "sexual morality" as the end all be all of marriage.

Jesus won't allow divorce for abuse

Also see:
Matthew 19:9
Mark 10:1-12
Luke 16:18

Matthew 5:39

*But I say unto you, That ye resist not evil: but **whosoever shall smite thee on thy right cheek, turn to him the other also.***

Jesus' command in this verse is to roll over and to submit to evil. This is the same defeatist attitude that Jesus has when he gives his (in)famous Sermon on the Mount, when he teaches people to accept their hunger, accept their poverty, and accept their sorrow (*Matthew 5:3-12*).

Contrary to what Jesus teaches, we should not turn our cheek to evil unless we are secretly planning to sneak up on evil and overthrow it with all of our might. We should always fight for what is right and what is fair and never accept defeat.

Jesus wants you to accept the evils of the world

Matthew 5:48

Be ye therefore perfect, *even as your Father which is in heaven is perfect.*

Jesus commands us to do something here that is impossible - be perfect.

Jesus will never accept us

Matthew 6:25-26

²⁵ *Therefore I say unto you,* **Take no thought for your life**, *what ye shall eat, or what ye shall drink; nor yet for your body, what ye shall put on. Is not the life more than meat, and the body than raiment?* ²⁶ *Behold the fowls of the air: for they sow not, neither do they reap, nor gather into barns; yet your heavenly Father feedeth them. Are ye not much better than they?*

In this passage, Jesus gives the horrible advice to not plan ahead for the future. He suggests that people should not think about procuring food or water. This is very easy for Jesus to say, since He can pull food out of nowhere whenever he wants (*Matthew 14:13-21*).

To prove his flawed point, Jesus points to the animal world, because he evidently believes that animals don't toil or worry. Jesus doesn't understand that the animals on the Earth spend all of their lives searching for food. The plants on the Earth die unless, as seeds, they're thrown into just the right micro-climate. The success of a few is only possible through the death of many.

Jesus doesn't want you to plan for the future

Matthew 7:6

Give not that which is holy unto the dogs, neither cast ye your pearls before swine, lest they trample them under their feet, and turn again and rend you.

Jesus hates dogs, and everyone knows that dogs are awesome. Clearly, Jesus has some judgment issues.

Jesus hates dogs

Matthew 7:12

Therefore all things *whatsoever ye would that men should do to you, do ye even so to them:* *for this is the law and the prophets.*

The Golden Rule

This verse, known as the Golden Rule, is often cited as an indication of Jesus' love and compassion. Jesus is essentially restating *Leviticus 19:18*, which says "love your neighbor as yourself," and *Leviticus 19:34* which commands the Israelites to treat their neighbors as they treat their own people.

The truth is that the Golden Rule is a terrible rule to live by. And the fact that Jesus merely parrots the flawed rule without adapting it even slightly, means that He is not worthy of worship in the least.

In order for us to agree that the Golden Rule is flawed, we must agree on the fact that, for the most part, gaining another person's consent is one of the most important components when figuring out if something is morally good or bad. (I'm not going to get into issues regarding consent with raising children, because that requires a much longer and more nuanced discussion.)

To illustrate why the Golden Rule is not based on consent and so not morally good, I want to tell a story that I heard many years ago when I was a boy:

> *There was a husband and wife who have been married for many years. Throughout those years, whenever the wife was sick, the husband would dote on her and constantly make sure she had everything she needed. However, whenever the husband was sick, the wife would leave him alone to himself, rarely checking in on him.*

> *One day, after many years, the husband finally asked his wife why she never doted on him when he was sick, as he had done for her. She was surprised, and told him that she didn't realize he wanted to be doted on. In fact, she told him that she didn't like to be doted on when she was sick, and that she was essentially treating her husband the way she wanted to be treated if she were sick.*
>
> *The husband and wife both realized then, that each one was treating the other as they themselves wanted to be treated, which ensured that neither of them was happy.*

In this story, neither the husband nor the wife were striving to gain their partner's consent for how they wanted to be treated, yet, both were following the Golden Rule (treat the other as you want the other to treat you). This story clearly illustrates how following the Golden Rule can lead to less than desirable outcomes.

A slightly different version of the Golden Rule is one that is sometimes referred to as The Platinum Rule, which essentially states:

> *treat others the way they want to be treated.*

While many argue that the Golden Rule and the Platinum rule are very similar, there is one huge fundamental component that is present in the Platinum Rule that is not present in the Golden Rule: consent. The Golden Rule is based on the ego, and talks about oneself. The Platinum Rule is based on consent, and talks about the other outside of oneself.

If the couple in the story followed the Platinum Rule rather than the Golden Rule, the husband would have asked the wife how she wanted to be treated when she was sick, and the wife would have asked the husband the same. Following the Platinum Rule and thereby gaining consent, both the husband and wife would have had much better experiences while they were sick.

While the story above is benign, the difference is easier understood in terms of masochism. Since a masochist desires pain, a masochist can inflict pain on others and still follow the Golden Rule. The masochist cannot do so with the Platinum Rule, since he would have to ask the other how he wanted to be treated.

From this, I argue that Jesus' dangerous words here have led to a society that doesn't value or understand consent, and ultimately lead to the Steubenville, Ohio incident in 2012, in which a number of High School students raped an unconscious girl. A paraphrase from the legal defense of the rapists in this case was:

> *She was unconscious so she didn't say no, and the absence of a "no" is equal to consent.*

If we consider that the boys in this case could have wanted a girl to have sex with them while they were passed out, then we could say that they were actually following the Golden Rule. We could not say the same in regards to the Platinum Rule.

Often when I bring this issue up, people respond that the Golden Rule was never meant to be read so literally, and that consent is implied. But if the Golden Rule is imperfect and can be restated as the Platinum Rule to produce a better understood law, then why choose the former? Why perpetuate a morality based on an individual's ego rather than the other person?

When you base your morality on the Golden Rule of Jesus, you forget entirely about the other person's own desires, and you only think of yourself. If you base your morality on the Platinum Rule, however, then you must always gain that consent from any other person you are dealing with.

Jesus does not understand consent

See also:
Luke 6:31

Matthew 7:13

Enter ye in at the strait gate: *for wide is the gate, and broad is the way, that leadeth to destruction, and many there be which go in thereat:*

Jesus is criticizing doing things the easy way in this verse. Sometimes it is the case that the easy way is the wrong way. But sometimes, the easy way can be the most fun and the most practical solution. Should we be worried that getting to Heaven isn't fun?

Additionally, in *Luke 13:24*, we read:

> *Strive to enter in at the strait gate: for many, I say unto you, will seek to enter in, and shall not be able.*

Here, Jesus plainly states that people are seeking to enter, and that they will not be able to. These are people who are actively seeking to enter, not people who don't care about entering. And Jesus is going to stop them from coming into the realm of Heaven, and likely cast them into the perpetually burning fires of Hell.

Unfortunately, as you have gleaned from this book, it is probably because Jesus' own words are completely confusing that people might not understand how to get through the gates.

Jesus will throw believers into Hell

See also:
Luke 13:22-24

Matthew 7:16-17

¹⁶*Ye shall know them by their fruits.* ***Do men gather grapes of thorns, or figs of thistles?*** **¹⁷***Even so every good tree bringeth forth good fruit; but a corrupt tree bringeth forth evil fruit.*

Jesus here is suggesting that "thorns" and "thistles" are bad and will only produce fruit of poor nature. This is also very bad advice - has Jesus not heard of raspberries or blackberries, which grow on thorny plants?

Jesus thinks raspberries are bad

Matthew 7:22 - 23

²²*Many will say to me in that day, Lord, Lord, have we not prophesied in thy name? and in thy name have cast out devils? and in thy name done many wonderful works?* **²³***And then will I profess unto them, I never knew you: depart from me, ye that work iniquity.*

Jesus is being very specific here about what he does not value: He doesn't value spreading prophesy, he doesn't' value healing people from demons; He doesn't even value the good works that people do in His name.

This means that all of those missions trips that good Christian teens go on are pointless in the eyes of Jesus. He doesn't even care. He will look those kids in their eyes when they die, and if they were not perfect in life, he will lie and say that he doesn't know them.

The other real issue here is that Jesus doesn't really take a moment to remind us what it is that we actually have to do to get into Heaven. Whether or not you believe that Jesus opened the door to Heaven, you hopefully can understand that he did a great job of opening the door to have hundreds if not thousands of interpretations of how to get into Heaven.

Jesus will send good people to Hell

Luke 14:26

*If any man come to me, and hate not his father, and mother, and wife, and children, and brethren, and sisters, yea, and his own life also, **he cannot be my disciple.***

While the original word in the text for "hate" may actually have been less harsh than today's meaning, it is clear that Jesus wants his followers to be ready to drop all ties with family at a moment's notice.

Jesus wants you to leave your family

Matthew 10:28

And fear not them which kill the body, but are not able to kill the soul: but rather **fear him which is able to destroy both soul and body in hell.**

Jesus is reminding us in this passage that we should be afraid of God. He isn't talking about a "respect" fear in this case, as apologists often try to argue.

If Jesus was telling us that we should respect God, He wouldn't reference someone who would kill you. If Jesus was talking about "respect", He would have stated something like, "respect not them who acquire great wealth, but not able to purchase immortality..."

Instead, Jesus references the terror-inducing concept of murder. He tells us that the fear we should have for God should be much more than the fear we should have for someone who would murder us.

Just in case we are not convinced, Jesus ends the verse reminding us that he is capable and more than ready to tortured us forever by having us burned alive in Hell.

Jesus wants you to be afraid of Him

See also:
Luke 12:4-5

Matthew 10:33

But whosoever shall deny me before men, **him will I also deny before my Father** *which is in heaven.*

The unfortunate part here is that we now know that poor Peter, Jesus' rock, the first Pope, is suffering in Hell at this very moment, since he did in fact deny Jesus before men (*Luke 22:54-62*).

At the risk of repeating myself, I feel compelled to remind the reader that to assess the nature of Jesus, we have to realize how much Jesus has worked to hide who He is from us: He spoke cryptically and esoterically, He never clearly responded to the Pharisees, He refused to prove Himself to those who asked, He hid in the desert to avoid people, and He refused to testify who He was to authorities.

Yet He will punish us for not believing that He is who He fails to prove Himself to be.

The other takeaway from this passage is that Jesus is acting very petty in this case. Jesus is the perfect being, the one who knows all and can do all. We are the imperfect, fallible human beings. Yet if we, in all of our failings, decide to deny Him, then He, the all-knowing, will deny us.

We are damned to base all of our beliefs on the limited knowledge we have. What is Jesus' excuse?

Jesus is petty

See also:
Luke 12:8-9

Mathtttew 10: 37-38

³⁷ He that loveth father or mother more than me is not worthy of me: and he that loveth son or daughter more than me is not worthy of me. ³⁸ And he that taketh not his cross, and followeth after me, is not worthy of me.

In case you weren't sure, Jesus wants you to forsake your family in order to follow a religious belief. I repeat: you should put your religious dogma above supporting your family.

This concept is very popular with many cults, such as Scientology, Fundamentalist Mormon movements, and even the Manson Family. The International Cultic Studies Association (ICSA) states "subservience to the leader or group requires members to cut ties with family and friends..." Cults will strategically manipulate potential deserters by replacing their actual families with their "new" family - other members in the cult.

Today when we hear of cults controlling people through with this mind-control practice, or even when we hear stories of people abandoning their family members because of religious beliefs, we must understand that Jesus would support that unscrupulous practice.

Jesus supports mind-control cults

See also:
Mathew 16:24-28

Matthew 12:47-50

⁴⁷*Then one said unto him, Behold, thy mother and thy brethren stand without, desiring to speak with thee.* **⁴⁸***But he answered and said unto him that told him,* ***Who is my mother? and who are my brethren?*** **⁴⁹***And he stretched forth his hand toward his disciples, and said, Behold my mother and my brethren!* **⁵⁰***For whosoever shall do the will of my Father which is in heaven, the same is my brother, and sister, and mother.*

While Jesus is preaching to people, His mom and family come to talk to Him. Jesus takes the opportunity to reinforce the idea that our real family should not be important to us. Rather, the people in our religion should replace our family.

In *Matthew 10:37-38*, Jesus tells his followers about abandoning their family members for the religion. But here in *Matthew 12:47-50*, Jesus actually practices what He preaches, showing how important his mind-control practice really is.

Be ready to abandon your family

See also:
Mark 3:21-35
Luke 8:19-21

Matthew 13:12

For whosoever hath, to him shall be given, and he shall have more abundance: but whosoever hath not, from him shall be taken away even that he hath.

In opposition to any previous message that Jesus may have stated, something like "the first shall be last and the last shall be first", Jesus is now rewarding people who have, and is now penalizing those who have not.

This is a case of Jesus supporting the idea of the rich getting richer and the poor getting poorer. This shouldn't be too surprising for the reader, since this book shows that Jesus doesn't really care about solving the issue of poverty anyway, and that Jesus believes we don't really need to spend too much worry over helping the poor, since there will always be poverty with us (*Matthew 26:11-13*).

Jesus steps on those who are down

Matthew 13:41-42

⁴¹ *The Son of man shall send forth his angels, and they shall gather out of his kingdom all things that offend, and them which do iniquity;* ⁴² *And shall cast them into a furnace of fire:* **there shall be wailing and gnashing of teeth.**

Jesus and God can easily snuff out evil forever. Instead, They are going to make offenders suffer horrible perpetually torturous deaths, complete with wailing and gnashing of teeth.

Jesus and God have such humanly devilish revenge fantasies.

Jesus is devilishly vengeful

See also:
Matthew 13:47-52

John 5:14

Afterward Jesus findeth him in the temple, and said unto him, Behold, thou art made whole: **sin no more, lest a worse thing come unto thee.**

Directly after Jesus heals a man, He tells him to sin no more, insinuating that it was the man's own sin that caused him his infirmity.

Actually, it is really God's structure of how the universe works, how reproductive biology works, that is the cause of this man's blindness. Jesus then, is blaming someone else for his Father's failures.

Jesus blames others for His Father's faults

John 12:24-25

²⁴*Verily, verily, I say unto you, Except a corn of wheat fall into the ground and die, it abideth alone: but if it die, it bringeth forth much fruit.* ²⁵ **He that loveth his life shall lose it;** *and he that hateth his life in this world shall keep it unto life eternal.*

First, let's deal with Jesus' fundamental misunderstanding of biology. Yes, the grain of wheat falls, but it doesn't die. In fact, it's the complete opposite: the grain of the wheat is the essence of its life. Also, the plant itself does not die due to the loss of grains, it is merely the reproductive system.

Regardless of Jesus' misunderstanding of biology, His message is awful: don't care about your life; don't make your life better; only focus on the hereafter. This is fine for Jesus, who is about to die, but for anyone with a family, Jesus' advice should be ignored.

Matthew's version of this passage (*Matthew 16:24*) adds, "Then said Jesus unto his disciples, If any man will come after me, let him deny himself, and take up his cross, and follow me." Even though Jesus came to sacrifice his own life for us, he still wants all of his followers to suffer by taking up a cross, just as Jesus will.

It is this kind of thinking that leads people to not care about eradicating poverty, hunger, and tragedy, none of which are even important to Jesus. Nowhere does Jesus indicate that he is concerned with people living a decent life on Earth.

Don't value your life

See also:
Mark 8:34-38
Luke 9:23-27
John 12:24-25

Luke 17:32-33

³²*Remember Lot's wife.* ³³**Whosoever shall seek to save his life shall lose it;** and **whosoever shall lose his life shall preserve it.**

In case you ever thought your family or your friends were important, Jesus wants you to know that you should be ready to turn your back on them in an instant in order to get into Heaven and avoid eternal torture.

At first, this passage seems benign, but Jesus references Lot's wife from the story of Sodom from *Genesis 19*. I've always found the story of Lot's wife intriguing. After all, it was Lot who thought that offering up his young daughters to a vicious mob was a good idea. Lot's wife's sin was being concerned with her family who she thinks is going to die. For Lot's sin - God cares nothing. For his wife's sin - she is killed instantly.

In order to understand Lot's wife's actions, we need to think empathetically about the story. After the angels tell Lot and his family that they are going to destroy Sodom, Lot's sons-in-law didn't believe them and so stay behind. As the angels drag the family away, Lot's wife turns to look back. Her sons are going to die, and she wants to mourn. For this, she is wasted.

Here in *Juke 17:32-33*, Jesus is reminding us not to be the kind of person who will even think about our family as he destroys our world. This is slightly odd compared to the story of the Prodigal Son, where a father rejoices when his son returns. Evidently, rejoicing when a son returns is good, worrying about and thinking about a son before that return can send you to hell.

Jesus wants you to disregard your family

Mark 8:38

Whosoever therefore shall be ashamed of me and of my words in this adulterous and sinful generation; ***of him also shall the Son of man be ashamed****, when he cometh in the glory of his Father with the holy angels.*

Evidently, God and Jesus are just as weak and spiteful as human beings, vowing to offer shame in return for shame.

I am still amazed that after all of the work Jesus is doing to not be believed by people, that He is still surprised when people don't believe in Him. He must be a weak being, fathered by a weak God, void of compassion.

Jesus is petty

See also:
Luke 9:26

Matthew 18:1-3

¹*At that time the disciples came to Jesus, saying, "Who is the greatest in the kingdom of heaven?"* ²*And calling to him a child, he put him in the midst of them* ³*and said, "Truly, I say to you,* **unless you turn and become like children, you will never enter the kingdom of heaven.**

I include this quote in this collection because it is one of the many times that Jesus speaks very cryptically to people who ask questions. If we believe that Heaven is real, then this is a very important aspect of getting into Heaven that we need to understand.

But how should one be like a child? Should one just believe in ridiculous things? Should one tell pee and poop jokes? Jesus is never clear on the matter, so we have to assume that Jesus didn't really care whether people made it to Heaven or burned forever in the fires of Hell.

In the following line, *Matthew 18:4*, Jesus states:

> *Whoever humbles himself like this child is the greatest in the kingdom of heaven.*

Jesus tells us here how to be the great once we make it into Heaven (by humbling oneself like a child), but we don't yet (or ever) know what it is about a child we must be like, in order to ensure our actual entrance.

Jesus wants to confuse you

See also:
Mark 10:15
Luke 18:17

Mark 9:42

And whosoever shall offend one of these little ones that believe in me, **it is better for him that a millstone were hanged about his neck***, and he were cast into the sea.*

In this verse, Jesus tells you what he may, in fact, do to the dear author of this book, if this book ends up turning anyone away from Him.

Jesus is going out of his way to describe the torture that he has been planning for people like me. Not only has he been considering hanging millstones around our necks and casting us into the sea, but he has also been considering and planning for even worse punishments!

Jesus plots psychopathic torture scenarios

Matthew 18:17

If he refuses to listen to them, tell it to the church. And if he refuses to listen even to the church, **let him be to you as a Gentile and a tax collector.**

In this verse, Jesus is instructing what to do if your brother sins against you, and if you confront him.

But the important part is at the end, when Jesus references Gentiles and tax collectors. Jesus is telling us how to treat people if we work very hard at establishing a relationship with our brother who sins against us. After we have exhausted all of the possible ways to rekindle our relationship, Jesus suggests that we sever all ties with the person, hence, treat him like a Gentile or tax collector.

This passage makes it clear that Jesus doesn't consider the gentiles or the tax collectors worthy of being treated humanely. Jesus shows us here that he does hate people, and that he does advocate treating some people like second- or third-class citizens.

Jesus allows treating some people with disdain

Matthew 19:21

*Jesus said to him, "**If you would be perfect, go, sell what you possess and give to the poor,** and you will have treasure in heaven; and come, follow me."*

After a man asks Jesus how to gain eternal life, Jesus tells him to follow certain commandments. But upon learning that the man already did what Jesus suggested, Jesus moves the goal posts and tells him one more condition, to sell all he had.

Selling all of your possessions to wander around with Jesus is very bad advice. Mostly because when His followers wander from town to town, they end up begging for food to eat, and they need to rely on strangers for lodging.

This story clearly shows Jesus moving the goal posts when it is convenient for Him, teaching us a valuable lesson: Jesus doesn't actually want us in Heaven. If He did want us in Heaven, he would clearly state how to get in, and he wouldn't keep changing the rules when he finds out certain people will gain admittance.

Ask any teacher what happens when you change a syllabus mid-semester, or when you change the rubrics of an assignment after students have already begun work. It de-motivates, confuses, and angers students because it unfairly punishes people who were trying to do their best.

Jesus doesn't want you in Heaven

Also see:
Mark 10:17-22
Luke 18:18-30

Matthew 19:29

And every one that hath forsaken houses, or brethren, or sisters, or father, or mother, or wife, or children, or lands, for my name's sake, shall receive an hundredfold, and shall inherit everlasting life.

In case any of Jesus' other messages about abandoning family are ambiguous, this verse should make it much more clear: Jesus encourages abandoning families - even children.

Jesus wants you to abandon family and children

See also:
Mark 10:28-31
Luke 18:28-30

Matthew 21:42-44

42 *Jesus saith unto them, Did ye never read in the scriptures, The stone which the builders rejected, the same is become the head of the corner: this is the Lord's doing, and it is marvellous in our eyes?* **43** *Therefore say I unto you, The kingdom of God shall be taken from you, and given to a nation bringing forth the fruits thereof.* **44 *And whosoever shall fall on this stone shall be broken: but on whomsoever it shall fall, it will grind him to powder.***

Jesus is again stating that non-believers are worthy of eternal suffering. In discussing the sins of the non-believers, Jesus focuses on hell, suffering, pain, and revenge.

There are a few other issues with this. First, Jesus is insinuating that everyone who rejects him deserves death. In this verse, Jesus is speaking to the Pharisees, and is essentially threatening them with killing them for not believing that He is Messiah. If the Pharisees at this point decide that they need to kill him, it is because Jesus is the aggressor.

Jesus threatens to kill people

See also:
Luke 20:17-18

Mark 13:7-8

⁷And when ye shall hear of wars and rumours of wars, be ye not troubled: **for such things must needs be;** *but the end shall not be yet.* ⁸*For nation shall rise against nation, and kingdom against kingdom: and there shall be earthquakes in divers places, and there shall be famines and troubles: these are the beginnings of sorrows.*

Jesus is telling us about how he makes plans for saving the world: wars; destruction; famine; and sorrow.

This is Jesus' gift to us. This is Jesus' good news to the world. If He wanted to, Jesus could easily bring peace to Earth in an instant. However, we know that Jesus likes to cause suffering, including but not limited to throwing people into burning hell-fire forever. So His plan of causing wars, destruction, famine, and sorrow actually make sense.

Jesus wants wars and destruction

Matthew 24:19

And woe unto them that are with child, and to them that give suck in those days!

Jesus is telling his disciples about what will happen when he comes again. This is part of Jesus' good news that he came to tell the world, regarding the new era of heaven on earth that Jesus will help bring forth.

The problem with this is that Jesus Himself acknowledges that he will bring destruction and other horrible things. He even knows that it will be horrible to anyone who is pregnant or nursing a small, innocent, defenseless child.

Again, this shows how little regard Jesus pays to the unborn and the newly-born. He is essentially saying that in order for him to come again, little children will suffer. He could make it such that when he comes, these little ones will miraculously be saved from suffering, but no, he wants to make them suffer.

Jesus wants children to suffer

See also:
Luke 21:22

Matthew 26:11-13

¹¹For ye have the poor always with you; *but me ye have not always.* **¹²***For in that she hath poured this ointment on my body, she did it for my burial.* **¹³***Verily I say unto you, Wheresoever this gospel shall be preached in the whole world, there shall also this, that this woman hath done, be told for a memorial of her.*

Jesus and his disciples are in Bethany in the house of Simon the Leper, and a woman decides to use some expensive oils to lavish upon Jesus. When Jesus' disciples see this, they realize that the expensive oils could instead be sold, so that the proceeds can be given away to the poor, as Jesus had instructed on previous occasions (such as *Matthew 19:21*).

When the disciples remind Jesus that He is not following His own rule, Jesus realizes he needs to make something up, so He decides that it is actually okay to be materialistic and extravagant because He's Jesus, after-all, and He's going to die soon.

However, the worst part of Jesus' message here is when He states, "ye have the poor always with you;" With this, Jesus lays the foundation for charities to choose band-aid solutions instead of trying to eradicate poverty altogether.

Jesus' thoughts on poverty are completely backward and unimpressive. He is okay with severe poverty existing. Otherwise, His teachings would include devising systems to eradicate poverty altogether.

Jesus wants poverty

See also:
Mark 14:3-9
John 12:1-8

Luke 23:27-31

27 *And there followed him a great company of people, and of women, which also bewailed and lamented him.* **28** *But Jesus turning unto them said, Daughters of Jerusalem, weep not for me,* **but weep for yourselves, and for your children.** **29** *For, behold, the days are coming, in the which they shall say, Blessed are the barren, and the wombs that never bare, and the paps which never gave suck.* **30** *Then shall they begin to say to the mountains, Fall on us; and to the hills, Cover us.* **31** *For if they do these things in a green tree, what shall be done in the dry?*

As people are weeping over Jesus' eventual demise, Jesus tries to comfort them by telling them that they had better save their weeping for later, when He sends destruction to torture people. For some reason, Jesus likes to torture. Remember, this is Jesus' good news.

Jesus is going to make life hell for pregnant and nursing women. Jesus is so distant from the reality of human being-ness that he thinks this will COMFORT the people he is talking to! He might as well say, "don't mourn for me, instead, mourn for yourselves when I'm going to come back and fuck you all up!"

Jesus looks forward to torturing people

John 15:6

If a man abide not in me, he is cast forth as a branch, and is withered; and men gather them, ***and cast them into the fire, and they are burned.***

Jesus loved talking about burning people alive - absolutely loved it. Does this worry anyone?

Remember, this is the same person who forces people to not believe in Him, purposefully speaks cryptically so that people can't understand Him, hides in the shadows so people cannot see Him, and avoids large crowds so He doesn't have to heal them.

But, if you don't believe in Him, you will be burned forever.

Jesus loves burning people alive

John 15:14

*Ye are my friends, **if ye do whatsoever I command you.***

Dear Jesus: Someone isn't your friend because they do what you tell them to do; and just because someone doesn't do what you command, that doesn't mean they aren't your friend.

This verse illuminates Jesus' psychopathy very well. Jesus actually thinks friendship is based on obeying commands. Many of us have had that friend when we were little - the one who bossed us around all Summer. And for some reason, we kept going back to play with this "friend" because we hadn't realized what true friendship was all about yet.

Then, one day, we stood up for ourselves and told our "friend" that we didn't want to do whatever our friend told us to do, and we suggested that we do something different - and suddenly our "friend" grew irate and threw us out and shouted that we were never friends in the first place.

So in this verse, Jesus just told you that that is exactly what He thinks friendship is. However, a few seconds later He realizes He sounds like a jerk, and He states in *John 15:17*:

These things I command you, that ye love one another.

But it's too late. We know what He thinks friendship is already.

Jesus is not your friend

John 16:12

I have yet many things to say unto you, *but ye cannot bear them now.*

Wait, Jesus! You told us about being tortured forever in fire, you told us about drinking human blood and eating human flesh...what didn't you think people could bear?

Unfortunately, we will never be able to hear what he has to say. Don't you hate when someone tells you that they can't tell you a secret they have? Well, thanks a lot, Jesus.

Jesus forgot to tell us important things

John 16:27

*For the Father himself loveth you, **because ye have loved me**, and have believed that I came out from God.*

Jesus is frank here when he reminds people that God didn't really love them from the start, and that God doesn't love people who don't believe in Jesus.

God's love is dependent on you loving Jesus

John 20:29

Jesus saith unto him, Thomas, because thou hast seen me, thou hast believed: **blessed are they that have not seen,** *and yet have believed.*

This quote comes right after Thomas asks to feel Jesus' wounds to make sure it is Him. Thomas wants to make sure he is worshiping the right God, since Jesus once suggested that there would be anti-Christs. In order to follow Jesus' wishes, Thomas may merely want to check Jesus' body.

But, rationality is thrown out of the window with Jesus, and instead, Jesus takes this opportunity to tell us that we should just believe anything, anywhere, any time, without verifying (or "seeing") first. This means we should believe Islam, Buddhism, and any other religious claim by anyone around the globe at any time.

This is a ridiculous notion that you can only use the full commandment: use rationality when evaluating OTHER religions use faith and fear of hell when evaluating MY religion.

Jesus doesn't want you to think

John 21:25

And there are also many other things which Jesus did, the which, if they should be written every one, I suppose that even the world itself could not contain the books that should be written. Amen.

It is funny that Jesus' Gospel is comprises less than a tenth of the length of the Old Testament, yet John seems to think it would be impossible or worthless to add any more to it.

This is either really good or really bad for Christianity. This could be bad because some of those things that Jesus did which weren't included in the Gospels could have helped people believe in Him and think him worthy of worship.

On the other hand, if the rest of the things Jesus did and said were as bad as the things cataloged in the Gospels, then maybe it was better for Jesus that they weren't written down.

It is important to note here that Jesus didn't even bother writing down what he did, or what he said. It must not have been that important to Jesus if his words were recorded. Or, perhaps more likely, it was Jesus' ultimate plan to burn as many people forever in Hell as he possibly could.

Jesus wants to burn people in Hell

VIII
The Parables

(Where we learn that Jesus really wants to torture unbelievers.)

Luke 12:13-21

The Parable of the Rich Fool

¹³*And one of the company said unto him, Master, speak to my brother, that he divide the inheritance with me.* ¹⁴*And he said unto him, Man, who made me a judge or a divider over you?* ¹⁵*And he said unto them, Take heed, and beware of covetousness: for a man's life consisteth not in the abundance of the things which he possesseth.*

¹⁶*And he spake a parable unto them, saying, The ground of a certain rich man brought forth plentifully:* ¹⁷*And he thought within himself, saying, What shall I do, because I have no room where to bestow my fruits?* ¹⁸*And he said, This will I do: I will pull down my barns, and build greater; and there will I bestow all my fruits and my goods.* ¹⁹*And I will say to my soul, Soul, thou hast much goods laid up for many years; take thine ease, eat, drink, and be merry.*

²⁰*But God said unto him,* **Thou fool, this night thy soul shall be required of thee: then whose shall those things be, which thou hast provided?** ²¹*So is he that layeth up treasure for himself, and is not rich toward God.*

Jesus tells a story whose message is: Don't prepare for the future; don't store up food to eat in the future; don't save money; don't invest in yourself.

Jesus' entire case for calling this man foolish rests on the fact that any one of us can die at any time. But so what? Does that mean we shouldn't prepare for our children or for other family members?

In the Old Testament, Joseph was able to secure a good position with the Pharaoh because he recommended that the Pharaoh store food for the future, just as the "fool" in Jesus' story did.

Overall, this shows us that Jesus doesn't value Joseph from the Old Testament, and doesn't want humans to live secure lives.

Jesus doesn't want you to prepare for the future

Matthew 6:25-34

The Fowls of the Air & the Lilies of the Field

25 *Therefore I say unto you,* **Take no thought for your life,** *what ye shall eat, or what ye shall drink; nor yet for your body, what ye shall put on. Is not the life more than meat, and the body than raiment?*

26 *Behold the fowls of the air: for they sow not, neither do they reap, nor gather into barns; yet your heavenly Father feedeth them. Are ye not much better than they?* **27** *Which of you by taking thought can add one cubit unto his stature?*

28 ***And why take ye thought for raiment?*** *Consider the lilies of the field, how they grow; they toil not, neither do they spin:* **29** *And yet I say unto you, That even Solomon in all his glory was not arrayed like one of these.* **30** *Wherefore, if God so clothe the grass of the field, which to day is, and to morrow is cast into the oven, shall he not much more clothe you, O ye of little faith?*

31 *Therefore take no thought, saying, What shall we eat? or, What shall we drink? or, Wherewithal shall we be clothed?* **32** *(For after all these things do the Gentiles seek:) for your heavenly Father knoweth that ye have need of all these things.* **33** *But seek ye first the kingdom of God, and his righteousness; and all these things shall be added unto you.*

34 ***Take therefore no thought for the morrow:*** *for the morrow shall take thought for the things of itself. Sufficient unto the day is the evil thereof.*

It is very easy for Jesus to tell people not to worry about eating because Jesus can create food whenever and wherever he wishes. Unlike many people in the world today, he doesn't have to worry about where his next meal will come from.

Instead of choosing to understand the plight of humanity, Jesus instead admonishes people for succumbing to the biological needs that he and His Father impose upon us.

Additionally, look at why he states that we shouldn't worry about food or clothing: God provides the birds and plants whatever they need.

First, God doesn't just provide for the birds. Birds work and toil all day long, like most wild animals. Very few animals actually live lives of comfort, and their lives usually consist of searching for food and avoiding predators.

Second, If God does in fact provide for the plants, then why don't people just automatically have food to eat like plants do? Instead of extracting resources from the earth and sun, humans actually do have to work hard to seek out and process all that our bodies need to survive.

There is another issue here, however, and it is that Jesus clearly doesn't understand humanity or any of animal- or plant-kind.

Jesus doesn't want you to prepare for your future

See also:
Luke 12:22–34

Matthew 13:3-9

The Parable of the Sower

[3] And he spake many things unto them in parables, saying, Behold, a sower went forth to sow; [4] And when he sowed, some seeds fell by the way side, and the fowls came and devoured them up: [5] Some fell upon stony places, where they had not much earth: and forthwith they sprung up, because they had no deepness of earth: [6] And when the sun was up, they were scorched; and because they had no root, they withered away. [7] And some fell among thorns; and the thorns sprung up, and choked them: [8] But other fell into good ground, and brought forth fruit, some an hundredfold, some sixtyfold, some thirtyfold. [9] Who hath ears to hear, let him hear.

Matthew 13:18-23

The Parable of the Sower Explained

[18] Hear ye therefore the parable of the sower. [19] When any one heareth the word of the kingdom, and understandeth it not, then cometh the wicked one, and catcheth away that which was sown in his heart. This is he which received seed by the way side. [20] But he that received the seed into stony places, the same is he that heareth the word, and anon with joy receiveth it; [21] Yet hath he not root in himself, but dureth for a while: for when tribulation or persecution ariseth because of the word, by and by he is offended. [22] He also that received seed among the thorns is he that heareth the word; and the care of this world, and the deceitfulness of riches, choke the word, and he becometh unfruitful. [23] But he that received seed into the good ground is he that heareth the word, and understandeth it; which also beareth fruit, and bringeth forth, some an hundredfold, some sixty, some thirty.

There are four types of people mentioned in this parable. First there are the seeds that fall to the wayside and are devoured. These represent people who are given the gospel but who don't understand it, and end up listening to their own hearts instead. "Liberal Christians" fall into this category because they read Jesus' ignorant and hateful words and instead imagine that Jesus is as kind as their own hearts.

Second, there are those that fall upon stony places, which spring up too soon and are scorched by the sun and wither. These seeds represent people who hear the word and like it, but when trouble comes they actually don't follow it, and abandon it.

Third, there are those that fall upon thorns and are choked to death. These seeds represent people who hear the Gospel but who live for riches. Mega-churches fall into this category, along with any church that accumulates wealth and luxury.

Last, there are those that fall upon good ground and bring forth fruit a hundredfold. These seeds represent people who hear the Gospel, understand it, and live it.

But Jesus leaves out a fifth group of seeds (people): The seeds that fall upon poor ground, and grow roots to reach good ground. These seeds overcome the poor soil to produce fruit a hundredfold. These seeds represent people who grew up in the Christian church who once believed Jesus was good and kind who shared wise words of advice. These people worked to understand the Jesus' words and realized He offered dangerous, ignorant, and hateful advice. These people are now free and much better off.

Jesus hides the most important seed

See also:
Mark 4:3-9
Mark 4:13-20

Mark 4:21-25

The Lesson of the Lamp

²¹*And he said unto them,* **Is a candle brought to be put under a bushel,** *or under a bed? and not to be set on a candlestick?* ²²*For there is nothing hid, which shall not be manifested; neither was any thing kept secret, but that it should come abroad.* ²³*If any man have ears to hear, let him hear.* ²⁴*And he said unto them, Take heed what ye hear: with what measure ye mete, it shall be measured to you: and unto you that hear shall more be given.* ²⁵*For he that hath, to him shall be given: and he that hath not, from him shall be taken even that which he hath.*

Jesus tells his followers about lamps, and asks them, "Is a candle brought to be put under a bushel, or under a bed?"

While Jesus is telling his followers this parable so that they will apply it to their own lives, so that they will not hide the truths they have received from Jesus, let us remember Jesus' own actions regarding hiding truths, from *John 7:3-4,*

> ³*His brethren therefore said unto him, Depart hence, and go into Judaea, that thy disciples also may see the works that thou doest.* ⁴*For there is no man that doeth any thing in secret, and he himself seeketh to be known openly. If thou do these things, shew thyself to the world.*

Jesus' response to His brothers' suggestion about not hiding his light under a bushel to let it shine for all to see was a big, fat, "NO." Jesus kept his light hid under a bushel for the entirety of His time on Earth, yet He mandates we do otherwise.

Jesus then issues a threat to anyone who may be hesitant to proclaim his message. His words about taking heed with "what measure ye mete," were designed to suggest to his followers that whomever does not proclaim Jesus' divinity will be tortured in Hell forever.

Jesus' threats of damnation never include instructing people to think, consider, or rationalize. Jesus consistently mandates that people come to His word as children - who do not have as much judgment or understanding as their adult counterparts. With Jesus, you either have to accept the entire story whole-heartedly without any doubt, or you will be burned alive forever in Hell.

Jesus hid his light under a bushel

See also:
Luke 8:16-18

Matthew 13:24-30

Parable of the Weeds

²⁴Another parable put he forth unto them, saying, The kingdom of heaven is likened unto a man which sowed good seed in his field: ²⁵But while men slept, his enemy came and sowed tares among the wheat, and went his way. ²⁶But when the blade was sprung up, and brought forth fruit, then appeared the tares also. ²⁷So the servants of the householder came and said unto him, Sir, didst not thou sow good seed in thy field? from whence then hath it tares? ²⁸He said unto them, An enemy hath done this. The servants said unto him, Wilt thou then that we go and gather them up? ²⁹But he said, Nay; lest while ye gather up the tares, ye root up also the wheat with them. ³⁰Let both grow together until the harvest: and in the time of harvest I will say to the reapers, **Gather ye together first the tares, and bind them in bundles to burn them:** but gather the wheat into my barn.

Matthew 13:36-43

Parable of the Weeds Explained

³⁶Then Jesus sent the multitude away, and went into the house: and his disciples came unto him, saying, Declare unto us the parable of the tares of the field. ³⁷He answered and said unto them, He that soweth the good seed is the Son of man; ³⁸The field is the world; the good seed are the children of the kingdom; but the tares are the children of the wicked one; ³⁹The enemy that sowed them is the devil; the harvest is the end of the world; and the reapers are the angels. ⁴⁰As therefore the tares are gathered and burned in the fire; so shall it be in the end of this world. ⁴¹**The Son of man shall send forth his angels, and they shall gather out of his kingdom all things that offend, and them which do iniquity;** ⁴²**And shall cast them into a furnace of fire: there shall be wailing and gnashing of teeth.** ⁴³Then shall the righteous shine forth as the sun in the kingdom of their Father. Who hath ears to hear, let him hear.

There are two issues that need to be considered when contemplating the parable of the weeds.

The first issue is how Jesus tells us he deals with sin and suffering. In this parable, Jesus tells us that He allows the sins of the world to take place without intervention (*let them grow together until the harvest*).

For some of us who live in the isolated wonders of modern civilization, this isn't so bad since most of the deeds of sinners we deal with are things such as bullying, theft, assaults, and other such deeds. It starts to get a little iffy when you consider murders and homicides - you might wonder why Jesus would choose to allow those sorts of sins to happen to us.

This is essentially "The Problem of Evil" or "The Problem of Suffering", which has been refuted by many apologists to some degree so I don't want to delve too much into that issue. But I do want to remind the reader that many of us don't contemplate on a daily basis that there are more heinous sins that are very troubling: sex-slavery, forced slave-labor, torture from murderous regimes, torture by religious fundamentalists, and much more. These sufferings are not only bad, but arguably even worse than Jesus' time on the cross, which he begged His father to allow Him to avoid.

Lastly, Jesus reminds us once again what his true love and passion are: burning people alive in Hell forever, so that there is much "wailing and gnashing of teeth."

Jesus allows torture on Earth, loves torture in Hell

See also:
Matthew 13:49-50

Matthew 13:44

The Parable of the Treasure

Again, the kingdom of heaven is like unto treasure hid in a field; **the which when a man hath found, he hideth***, and for joy thereof goeth and selleth all that he hath, and buyeth that field.*

Matthew 13:45-46

The Parable of the Pearl

⁴⁵Again, **the kingdom of heaven is like unto a merchant man, seeking goodly pearls***: ⁴⁶Who, when he had found one pearl of great price, went and sold all that he had, and bought it.*

The problem with Jesus' parables is that they present poor models to live by while on Earth. Here we have two examples of greed that are supposed to show us how to act properly to get into Heaven.

In the parable of the treasure, the analogy is that if you find a treasure hidden in a field, you should secretly purchase the field so that you can keep the treasure as your own. But that isn't the honest thing to do. When I find a wallet on the ground, I do not deviously try to obtain the wallet for my own gain. I will pick up the wallet in the open and try to find out who the owner is. If that fails, I will turn the wallet over to a lost-and-found, or to any authorities who may be able to return the property to its rightful owner.

Just as troubling, in the parable of the pearl, Jesus' example includes a man who greedily and single-mindedly sells all he has for one perfect pearl.

When investing one's money, it is commonly understood that diversification is very important in order to weather the ups and downs of the market. If you invest all of your wealth in one thing, then it is very possible you will lose all of your money at some point. (Jesus' parable of the pearl, then, actually shows that it is not a wise idea to invest in Heaven, if it is like a "pearl of great price").

Jesus rewards greed

Luke 16:19-31

The Parable of the Rich Man and Lazarus

¹⁹*There was a certain rich man, which was clothed in purple and fine linen, and fared sumptuously every day:* ²⁰*And there was a certain beggar named Lazarus, which was laid at his gate, full of sores,* ²¹*And desiring to be fed with the crumbs which fell from the rich man's table: moreover the dogs came and licked his sores.*

²²*And it came to pass, that the beggar died, and was carried by the angels into Abraham's bosom: the rich man also died, and was buried;* ²³*And in hell he lift up his eyes, being in torments, and seeth Abraham afar off, and Lazarus in his bosom.* ²⁴*And he cried and said, Father Abraham, have mercy on me, and send Lazarus, that he may dip the tip of his finger in water, and cool my tongue; for I am tormented in this flame.*

²⁵*But Abraham said, Son, remember that thou in thy lifetime receivedst thy good things, and likewise Lazarus evil things: but now he is comforted, and thou art tormented.* ²⁶*And beside all this, between us and you there is a great gulf fixed: so that they which would pass from hence to you cannot; neither can they pass to us, that would come from thence.*

²⁷*Then he said, I pray thee therefore, father, that thou wouldest send him to my father's house:* ²⁸*For I have five brethren; that he may testify unto them, lest they also come into this place of torment.* ²⁹*Abraham saith unto him, They have Moses and the prophets; let them hear them.*

³⁰*And he said, Nay, father Abraham: but if one went unto them from the dead, they will repent.* ³¹*And he said unto him,* ***If they hear not Moses and the prophets, neither will they be persuaded, though one rose from the dead.***

Fuck Jesus

The important part of this story is at the end when Abraham tells the rich man that if his brothers can't listen to the prophets, then what good would it do to listen to their dead brother's ghost warning them of impending doom.

To that, I say that this parable illuminates the complete idiocy of Jesus. Jesus believes that seeing a ghost who can show itself to be real is not as good as an old book of superstitious dead people. Jesus thinks that we are more likely to believe a very old book of ignorant ramblings than believe an apparition of a close loved one.

Not only is Jesus wrong on this, but we know that even Jesus doesn't believe His own words, and hence is lying to his followers and to us.

The Apostle Paul of Tarsus, Christianity's most important figure did not believe in the writings or stories of the Christians. He believed in the apparition of Jesus.

Jesus deceives you

Matthew 22:1-14

The Parable of the Banquet

¹*And Jesus answered and spake unto them again by parables, and said,* ²*The kingdom of heaven is like unto a certain king, which made a marriage for his son,* ³*And sent forth his servants to call them that were bidden to the wedding: and they would not come.*

⁴*Again, he sent forth other servants, saying, Tell them which are bidden, Behold, I have prepared my dinner: my oxen and my fatlings are killed, and all things are ready: come unto the marriage.* ⁵*But they made light of it, and went their ways, one to his farm, another to his merchandise:*

⁶*And the remnant took his servants, and entreated them spitefully, and slew them.* ⁷*But when the king heard thereof, he was wroth: and he sent forth his armies, and destroyed those murderers, and burned up their city.* ⁸*Then saith he to his servants, The wedding is ready, but they which were bidden were not worthy.* ⁹*Go ye therefore into the highways, and as many as ye shall find, bid to the marriage.* ¹⁰*So those servants went out into the highways, and gathered together all as many as they found, both bad and good: and the wedding was furnished with guests.*

¹¹*And when the king came in to see the guests, he saw there a man which had not on a wedding garment:* ¹²*And he saith unto him, Friend, how camest thou in hither not having a wedding garment? And he was speechless.* ¹³**Then said the king to the servants, Bind him hand and foot, and take him away, and cast him into outer darkness; there shall be weeping and gnashing of teeth.** ¹⁴*For many are called, but few are chosen.*

Jesus tells of a parable in which a king wants to force his people to come to his son's wedding. (I wonder how many of his subjects' weddings the King has attended.) It took him a few tries, but eventually the king found people who had the time to attend the ceremony.

The king then notices someone who isn't dressed appropriately, and the king believes this makes the man worthy of suffering in agony for all of eternity.

In the parable, there are murderers who don't receive the punishment reserved for the improper dresser - Jesus reserves the harshest judgment for someone who didn't wear "wedding clothes". This is the kind of person Jesus is, and this is the kind of person his Father in Heaven is.

Jesus' code of ethics are fundamentally flawed

Luke 14:16-24

The Parable of the Banquet

[16] *Then said he unto him, A certain man made a great supper, and bade many:* [17] *And sent his servant at supper time to say to them that were bidden, Come; for all things are now ready.* [18] *And they all with one consent began to make excuse. The first said unto him, I have bought a piece of ground, and I must needs go and see it: I pray thee have me excused.* [19] *And another said, I have bought five yoke of oxen, and I go to prove them: I pray thee have me excused.* [20] *And another said, I have married a wife, and therefore I cannot come.*

[21] *So that servant came, and shewed his lord these things. Then the master of the house being angry said to his servant, Go out quickly into the streets and lanes of the city, and bring in hither the poor, and the maimed, and the halt, and the blind.* [22] *And the servant said, Lord, it is done as thou hast commanded, and yet there is room.* [23] *And the lord said unto the servant, Go out into the highways and hedges, and compel them to come in, that my house may be filled.* [24] *For I say unto you,* **That none of those men which were bidden shall taste of my supper.**

In this version of the parable of the banquet, Jesus compares himself (and God) to a selfish arrogant prick who cannot empathize with people who have their own life events.

The man who has dinner to share with people thinks his dinner is more important than other people's needs to prepare and inspect property or a new husband's desire to spend quality time with his new wife.

Instead of issuing a rain-check, this man childishly states that they will never be asked to dine with him again.

Jesus is petulant

Matthew 25:1-13

The Parable of the Ten Virgins

¹*Then shall the kingdom of heaven be likened unto ten virgins, which took their lamps, and went forth to meet the bridegroom.* ²*And five of them were wise, and five were foolish.* ³*They that were foolish took their lamps, and took no oil with them:* ⁴*But the wise took oil in their vessels with their lamps.*

⁵*While the bridegroom tarried, they all slumbered and slept.* ⁶*And at midnight there was a cry made, Behold, the bridegroom cometh; go ye out to meet him.* ⁷*Then all those virgins arose, and trimmed their lamps.* ⁸*And the foolish said unto the wise, Give us of your oil; for our lamps are gone out.* ⁹*But the wise answered, saying, Not so; lest there be not enough for us and you: but go ye rather to them that sell, and buy for yourselves.*

¹⁰*And while they went to buy, the bridegroom came; and they that were ready went in with him to the marriage: and the door was shut.* ¹¹*Afterward came also the other virgins, saying, Lord, Lord, open to us.* ¹²*But he answered and said, Verily I say unto you, I know you not.* ¹³*Watch therefore,* **for ye know neither the day nor the hour wherein the Son of man cometh.**

In this parable, Jesus is telling a story about how Jesus is like the bridegroom who is going to marry ten women (where are all of the Christians who are arguing for this particular Jesus-sanctioned biblically-defined polygamous marriage?).

The foolish women in the story don't bring extra oil for their lamps. The smart women do bring extra oil. The women were evidently going to marry a huge jerk who didn't tell his finances when he was going to come to get them. He then punishes the women who don't supply themselves with enough oil to keep their lamps lit.

The problem here is that we are left wondering how much oil they actually should have brought for themselves. Should they have brought a day's supply? A week's supply? A month's supply? Jesus tells his followers that he is going to return soon, yet so far, it has been about two thousand years.

This shows that Jesus denies us the information necessary to plan ahead, but will punish us forever for not being ready.

Jesus sets us up for failure

Matthew 25:14-30

The Parable of the Talents

14 *For the kingdom of heaven is as a man travelling into a far country, who called his own servants, and delivered unto them his goods.* **15** *And unto one he gave five talents, to another two, and to another one; to every man according to his several ability; and straightway took his journey.* **16** *Then he that had received the five talents went and traded with the same, and made them other five talents.* **17** *And likewise he that had received two, he also gained other two.* **18** *But he that had received one went and digged in the earth, and hid his lord's money.*

19 *After a long time the lord of those servants cometh, and reckoneth with them.* **20** *And so he that had received five talents came and brought other five talents, saying, Lord, thou deliveredst unto me five talents: behold, I have gained beside them five talents more.* **21** *His lord said unto him, Well done, thou good and faithful servant: thou hast been faithful over a few things, I will make thee ruler over many things: enter thou into the joy of thy lord.*

22 *He also that had received two talents came and said, Lord, thou deliveredst unto me two talents: behold, I have gained two other talents beside them.* **23** *His lord said unto him, Well done, good and faithful servant; thou hast been faithful over a few things, I will make thee ruler over many things: enter thou into the joy of thy lord.*

24 *Then he which had received the one talent came and said, Lord, I knew thee that thou art an hard man, reaping where thou hast not sown, and gathering where thou hast not strawed:* **25** *And I was afraid, and went and hid thy talent in the earth: lo, there thou hast that is thine.*

26 *His lord answered and said unto him, Thou wicked and slothful servant, thou knewest that I reap where I sowed not, and gather where I have not strawed:* **27** *Thou oughtest therefore to have put my money to the exchangers, and then at my coming I should have received mine own with usury.* **28** *Take therefore the talent from him, and give it unto him which hath ten talents.*

29 *For unto every one that hath shall be given, and he shall have abundance: but from him that hath not shall be taken away even that which he hath.* **30** ***And cast ye the unprofitable servant into outer darkness: there shall be weeping and gnashing of teeth.***

Fuck Jesus

In this parable, Jesus uses an analogy about capitalistic investment to discuss the nature of Heaven.

Jesus gives us insight to his personality, however, through the words of the servant in the parable (Matthew 25:24):

> *Then he which had received the one talent came and said, Lord, I knew thee that thou art an hard man, reaping where thou hast not sown, and gathering where thou hast not strawed:*

Jesus tells us exactly who he is: He is a hard man who takes what isn't his, and who punishes people for not making a profit.

Jesus takes what isn't his

Luke 19: 12-27

The Parable of the Ten Minas

[12] *He said therefore, A certain nobleman went into a far country to receive for himself a kingdom, and to return.* [13] *And he called his ten servants, and delivered them ten pounds, and said unto them, Occupy till I come.* [14] *But his citizens hated him, and sent a message after him, saying, We will not have this man to reign over us.*

[15] *And it came to pass, that when he was returned, having received the kingdom, then he commanded these servants to be called unto him, to whom he had given the money, that he might know how much every man had gained by trading.*

[16] *Then came the first, saying, Lord, thy pound hath gained ten pounds.* [17] *And he said unto him, Well, thou good servant: because thou hast been faithful in a very little, have thou authority over ten cities.* [18] *And the second came, saying, Lord, thy pound hath gained five pounds.* [19] *And he said likewise to him, Be thou also over five cities.* [20] *And another came, saying, Lord, behold, here is thy pound, which I have kept laid up in a napkin:* [21] **For I feared thee, because thou art an austere man: thou takest up that thou layedst not down, and reapest that thou didst not sow.**

[22] *And he saith unto him, Out of thine own mouth will I judge thee, thou wicked servant. Thou knewest that I was an austere man, taking up that I laid not down, and reaping that I did not sow:* [23] *Wherefore then gavest not thou my money into the bank, that at my coming I might have required mine own with usury?*

[24] *And he said unto them that stood by, Take from him the pound, and give it to him that hath ten pounds.* [25] *(And they said unto him, Lord, he hath ten pounds.)* [26] *For I say unto you, That unto every one which hath shall be given; and from him that hath not, even that he hath shall be taken away from him.* [27] **But those mine enemies, which would not that I should reign over them, bring hither, and slay them before me.**

Fuck Jesus

Most atheists incorrectly attribute the last verse of this parable to Jesus in order to indicate how horrible Jesus is. But I think that's unfair, or at least premature.

Yes, this is a parable, and Jesus is merely quoting the words of a hypothetical nobleman who wants to see people die. As most Christians claim when hearing this, Jesus isn't actually ordering people to bring anyone to him to be killed, since those words are from someone in Jesus' story.

Jesus is, however, telling people about his fanatical wishes that will happen AFTER he becomes a supernatural king. Jesus is telling his followers that when He returns, then He will gladly call for those who did not believe in Him and have them slaughtered in front of Him.

Additionally, at the end of the parable, Jesus instructs that those who have, will have more. This may seem to contradict the first/last teachings of Jesus (Matthew 20:16), even if the "more" in this particular parable refers to faith and not material possessions.

What the nobleman is actually rewarding is a blind faith that his servants took in investing during a shaky market period. The nobleman is punishing those who intelligently withheld their investment during a time of change-over. (It is important to note that Jesus doesn't tell us what the nobleman would have done to a servant who lost his minas on choosing a poor investment.)

Lastly, Jesus tells us who he is: he is hard; he takes what he did not put in; and he reaps what he did not sow.

Jesus wants to torture unbelievers

IX
The Deception

(Where we learn that Jesus deliberately deceived people into unbelief.)

Matthew 11:25-27

25 *At that time Jesus answered and said, I thank thee, O Father, Lord of heaven and earth, because* **thou hast hid these things from the wise and prudent, and hast revealed them unto babes.** **26** *Even so, Father: for so it seemed good in thy sight.* **27** *All things are delivered unto me of my Father: and no man knoweth the Son, but the Father; neither knoweth any man the Father, save the Son, and he to whomsoever the Son will reveal him.*

Here Jesus is plainly stating that he has come to deceive. Specifically, he has come to deceive those who are wise and prudent, and that it is the ignorant who have received a revelation of the truth.

This should say something about Jesus and God: They do not respect intelligence and instead want people to remain in child-like ignorance. Jesus actively hides his identity from those who seek him, and He revels in confusing people.

Jesus wants you to be stupid

See also:
Luke 10:21-24

Matthew 13:10-11

10 *And the disciples came, and said unto him, Why speakest thou unto them in parables?* **11** *He answered and said unto them, Because it is given unto you to know the mysteries of the kingdom of heaven,* ***but to them it is not given.***

Jesus thinks human beings are idiots, so he belittles their intelligence by telling them childish stories instead of telling them the truth.

As an aside, Jesus doesn't realize that for the parables to be of any use, his followers would have to use their intelligence to apply the stories to their lives anyway.

Jesus hides the truth from his followers

See also:
Mark 4:10-12
Luke 8:9-10

John 12:37-41

³⁷*But though he had done so many miracles before them, yet they believed not on him:* ³⁸*That the saying of Esaias the prophet might be fulfilled, which he spake, Lord, who hath believed our report? and to whom hath the arm of the Lord been revealed?* ³⁹*Therefore they could not believe, because that Esaias said again,* ⁴⁰**He hath blinded their eyes, and hardened their heart; that they should not see with their eyes, nor understand with their heart,** *and be converted, and I should heal them.* ⁴¹*These things said Esaias, when he saw his glory, and spake of him.*

In case anyone is at all confused: Jesus does not want people to believe in Him. He blinds their eyes and hardens their hearts.

In other words, it is very likely that Jesus manipulates those who once believed, and forces them to not believe, so he can torture them forever.

Jesus forces people to disbelieve in Him

John 15:22-25

²²*If I had not come and spoken unto them, they had not had sin: but now they have no cloke for their sin.* ²³*He that hateth me hateth my Father also.* ²⁴*If I had not done among them the works which none other man did, they had not had sin: but now have they both seen and hated both me and my Father.* ²⁵*But this cometh to pass, that the word might be fulfilled that is written in their law,* **They hated me without a cause.**

In this passage, Jesus claims that he came to speak to us. However, as has been shown, Jesus speaks in secret, He speaks in code, He forces people to not believe Him, He doesn't follow scripture, He tells people that they have to think like a child (don't use judgment) in order to understand him, and Jesus thinks that He has made his case good enough for us to believe him, and that we are worthy of eternal torture if we don't.

Jesus is suggesting that there was nothing more that he could have done to get people to believe in Him, as if He didn't consider telling people the truth. Remember, he's going to torture people forever because of whether or not they believe in him, and he consistently and actively fails to convince.

The other irony is that if Jesus had just not come down, people wouldn't be burning forever in hell because they decide to use their brains. Jesus adds nothing to the theology, and instead brings with him a philosophy of perpetual damnation.

Jesus doesn't understand the power of the truth

John 16:25

These things have I spoken unto you in proverbs: but the time cometh, **when I shall no more speak unto you in proverbs, but I shall shew you plainly of the Father**

Apparently, Jesus decides that the best time to actually tell people about God is right before he dies. He spends the majority of his teaching career using esoteric language, odd stories, and confusing analogies, yet is saving clear and plain language for last. Unfortunately, Jesus once again shows he is a liar, since he never uses the plain language which he promises here.

Additionally, directly after Jesus tells his disciples that he will some day use plain language, they respond that they now believe him because he is using plain language.

Either His disciples are slower than even Jesus gives them credit for, or the writers of the Gospels completely failed to write down the most important part - the explanation of the nature of God and Heaven in plain language!

Jesus intends to confuse

Matthew 27:11

And Jesus stood before the governor: and the governor asked him, saying, Art thou the King of the Jews? ***And Jesus said unto him, Thou sayest.***

Jesus is now in the last stages of his plan: He has been caught and is now going to be punished by the authorities, just as He planned for.

The really annoying part of this is that Jesus still cannot actually say whether or not he is the King of the Jews. If he is actually the King of the Jews, he could say, "Am I the King of the Jews? Verily, verily I tell you that yes, I am. That's what I've been trying to tell all of you people for the longest time!"

Instead, Jesus continues to confuse and deceive by retorting a childish phrase similar to "I know you are but what am I?"

Jesus avoids honesty

Luke 22:66-70

66And as soon as it was day, the elders of the people and the chief priests and the scribes came together, and led him into their council, saying, **67**Art thou the Christ? tell us. And he said unto them, If I tell you, ye will not believe: **68**And if I also ask you, ye will not answer me, nor let me go. **69**Hereafter shall the Son of man sit on the right hand of the power of God. **70**Then said they all, Art thou then the Son of God? **And he said unto them, Ye say that I am.**

Remember that Jesus' own plan from the very beginning has been to get caught and become killed by authorities. Now that he is at the very end of his plan, He can easily state who he is. Instead, Jesus continues to remain silent, in order to confuse people.

Jesus avoids honesty

Luke 23:3

And Pilate asked him, saying, Art thou the King of the Jews? ***And he answered him and said, Thou sayest it.***

Again, we see yet another example of Jesus avoiding honesty in order to conceal who he is.

Jesus avoids honesty

John 18:37

Pilate therefore said unto him, Art thou a king then? Jesus answered, **Thou sayest that I am a king.** *To this end was I born, and for this cause came I into the world, that I should bear witness unto the truth. Every one that is of the truth heareth my voice.*

Jesus is so concerned that people believe Him, but at one of the most important times in His life, He chooses not to answer a very direct question. He is going to die, and remains either a coward, or a deceptive jerk.

This passage is the closest we ever get to Jesus admitting openly that He is the King of the Jews, yet Jesus' response isn't even very assertive. Instead of stating that He was indeed the King of Jews, Jesus instead throws the question back into Pilate's face and remains esoteric by saying, "Thou sayest that I am a king..."(And actually, Pilate never said he was a king - Pilate asked if He said that He Himself was a king.)

Jesus claims to care about the truth, yet Jesus never tries to openly or convincingly show us who he is. Instead, He spends his entire ministry lying to and hiding from His followers, avoiding those who need Him, admonishing those who love Him, and threatening those who believe in Him.

Jesus is a deceptive, psychopathic liar

X
The Index

A

abandon 55
adultery 87, 89
angel(s) 13, 14, 18
anger 59, 86
annointing 119

B

banquet, parable of 142, 144, 145
barren wombs 120
blackberries 98
blasphamy 73
blindness 53, 61, 107
boat 37
bread 39
burial 36
bushel 134, 135

C

Canaanite 56
candle 134, 135
Catch-22 29, 30
chaff 17
child-bride 13
children 111
compassion 50
confusion 34, 39
corn 22
corner stone 116
cross 108
cult 103

D

David 22
deafness 53
death penalty 22, 25
deception 28
demon(s) 49, 56
denial 102
desert 18
despise 70
destruction 117
diarrhea 26
dinner 144, 145
disabled 61
divorce 32, 89
dog(s) 56, 93
doubt 60

E

Elijah 18
enter kingdom like a child 111
exorcism 49, 99

F

faith 37, 38, 41, 42, 43, 51
family
  abandon 36, 68, 100, 103, 104
  disown 19, 68, 74, 103, 104
  disregard 14, 16, 19, 36, 68, 109
famine 117
fear 101
feeding the hungry 58
fig (tree) 59
fire 17, 121
fool 86
fornication 89
friendship 122
fruit 98

G

gate 97
generations 12
Gentile 113
germs 26
gnashing of teeth 106, 136, 137, 148
God's love 124
Golden Rule 94
greed 139

H

hate 68, 100
healing 48, 50, 52, 54
heaven
  gaining entry 114
hell 33
Herod 14
Holy Ghost 13, 73
hungry 76, 83, 84

I

issue of blood 51

J

John the Baptist 17, 18
Jonas 23
Joseph 12, 13, 16
jot 85
Judas 40, 44, 45, 77

K

kill
  bride 13
  children 14, 52
  disciples 67
  false prophets 28
King of the Jews 14

L

lamp, The lesson of the 134, 135
laughter 83, 84
Lazarus, parable of the rich man and 140, 141
lepers 48, 53
light 134, 135
Lilies (of the field) 130
lineage 12
Lot 109
Lot's wife 109
love 124
lust 87

M

marriage 13, 19, 32, 89, 146
Mary 12, 13, 16, 19, 74
meek 71
millstone 112
minas, parable of the ten 150
mind-control 103, 104
Moses 18, 30, 32, 48
murder 13, 14
mustard seed 42

N

non-Jews 56, 64

O

ointment 119

P

parables 155
pearl 138
perfection 91
persecution 67
Peter 38, 40, 102
Pharisees 22, 23, 25, 26, 27, 32
pigs 49
Pilate 161, 162
poor in spirit 82
poor planning 13
poverty 53, 105, 119
prepare 128, 129, 131
Problem of Evil, the 137

R

raising the dead 50
raspberries 98
respect 101
resurrection 60
revenge 106
riches 114, 128

S

Sabbath 22, 24
Satan 18, 40, 44, 45
scripture 29
seeds 132, 133
serpent 79
sign 23, 27, 31, 80
sin 61
Slaughter of the Innocents 14
snake 79
Sodom and Gomorrha 66, 109
sorrow 82, 117
Sower, parable of the 132, 133
speaking plainly 39
stone 116
storm 37, 38
strait gate 97
submit to evil 90
suffering
  of children 118
  of nursing women 118
  of pregnant women 118
swine 49
syllabus 114

T

tares 136
tax collector 113
thistles 98
Thomas, doubting 125
thorns 98
thought-crime(s) 86, 87
tittle 85
torture 17, 112, 120, 135
treasure 138

U

unbelievers 66, 75
undesireables 48
unquenchable fire 17

V

virgin 13
virgins, parable of the ten 146
vision 14

W

war 117
washing hands 26
water
  walking on 38
wedding 19, 142
weeds 136
weeping 120
wheat 108
wind 38
wine 19
wise men 14
woman 19
working on Sabbath 22, 24
works 99

Y

yoke 71, 72

Fuck Jesus

Made in the USA
Columbia, SC
08 February 2021